Raspberry Pi Robotics Essentials

Harness the power of Raspberry Pi with Six Degrees of Freedom (6DoF) to create an amazing walking robot

Richard Grimmett

PUBLISHING

BIRMINGHAM - MUMBAI

Raspberry Pi Robotics Essentials

First published: June 2015

Production reference: 1150615

Published by Packt Publishing Ltd.
Livery Place
35 Livery Street
Birmingham B3 2PB, UK.

ISBN 978-1-78528-484-7

www.packtpub.com

Credits

Author
Richard Grimmett

Reviewers
Ashwin Pajankar
Werner Ziegelwanger

Commissioning Editor
Neil Alexander

Acquisition Editor
Tushar Gupta

Content Development Editor
Kirti Patil

Technical Editor
Mahesh Rao

Copy Editors
Aditya Nair
Sameen Siddiqui
Stuti Srivastava

Project Coordinator
Kranti Berde

Proofreader
Safis Editing

Indexer
Priya Sane

Graphics
Sheetal Aute

Production Coordinator
Shantanu N. Zagade

Cover Work
Shantanu N. Zagade

About the Author

Richard Grimmett has more fun working on robotic projects than should be allowed. He also enjoys teaching computer science and electrical engineering at Brigham Young University, Idaho. He has a bachelor's and master's degree in electrical engineering and a PhD in leadership studies. He has written books on how to use Raspberry Pi, Arduino, and BeagleBone Black for robotics projects.

About the Reviewers

Ashwin Pajankar is a Bangalore-based engineer who wears many different hats depending on the occasion. He graduated from IIIT Hyderabad in 2012 with a master of technology degree in computer science and engineering. He has a total of 5 years of experience in the software industry, where he has worked in different domains, such as testing, data warehousing, replication, and automation. He is very well versed in DB concepts, SQL, and scripting with Bash and Python. He has earned professional certifications in products from Oracle, IBM, Informatica, and Teradata. He's also an ISTQB-certified tester.

In his free time, he volunteers for different technical hackathons or social-service activities. He was introduced to the Raspberry Pi in one of the hackathons, and he's been hooked on it ever since. He writes a lot of code in Python, C, C++, and Shell on his Raspberry Pi B+ cluster. He's currently working on creating his own Beowulf cluster of 64 Raspberry Pi 2 models.

Werner Ziegelwanger, MSc, has studied game engineering and simulation, and he got his master's degree in 2011. His master's thesis was published with the title *Terrain Rendering with Geometry Clipmaps for Games*, by Diplomica Verlag. His hobbies include programming and games and working with all kinds of technical gadgets.

Werner was a self-employed programmer for some years and mainly worked on Web projects. During this time, he started his own blog (`http://developer-blog.net`), which is about the Raspberry Pi, Linux, and open source.

Since 2013, Werner has been working as a Magento developer and the head of programming at mStage GmbH, an eCommerce company focused on Magento.

www.PacktPub.com

Support files, eBooks, discount offers, and more

For support files and downloads related to your book, please visit www.PacktPub.com.

Did you know that Packt offers eBook versions of every book published, with PDF and ePub files available? You can upgrade to the eBook version at www.PacktPub.com and as a print book customer, you are entitled to a discount on the eBook copy. Get in touch with us at service@packtpub.com for more details.

At www.PacktPub.com, you can also read a collection of free technical articles, sign up for a range of free newsletters and receive exclusive discounts and offers on Packt books and eBooks.

https://www2.packtpub.com/books/subscription/packtlib

Do you need instant solutions to your IT questions? PacktLib is Packt's online digital book library. Here, you can search, access, and read Packt's entire library of books.

Why subscribe?

- Fully searchable across every book published by Packt
- Copy and paste, print, and bookmark content
- On demand and accessible via a web browser

Free access for Packt account holders

If you have an account with Packt at www.PacktPub.com, you can use this to access PacktLib today and view 9 entirely free books. Simply use your login credentials for immediate access.

Table of Contents

Preface

There have been many recent technological advances that have really changed the way we live, work, and play. The television, the computer, and the cell phone all have dramatically affected our lives. Each of these generally started out with a few early adopters, for the most part, individuals with lots of resources that were able to afford the new technology. However, soon after, there was a movement to make the technology more affordable for a wider range of people.

The latest technological movement is robotics. The number, kind, and use of robots is growing dramatically. The first of these robots were developed in university labs or in military research centers. However, just as with the adaption of the computer, there is already a growing grassroots movement of do-it-yourself developers that has sprung up to make robots a part of our everyday life.

This movement has been fueled by inexpensive hardware and free, open source software. However, it has also been enabled by a community of developers who are willing to help others get started or overcome challenges that they have experienced.

This book is offered in the spirit of this do-it-yourself movement. Inside the book, you'll find details about how to take Raspberry Pi B 2, an inexpensive, small, but versatile computer, and marry it with inexpensive hardware and open source software to build a bipedal robot that can walk, sense barriers, and even see its surroundings.

However, be careful—this sort of information can be dangerous. Before long, you may be creating the next generation of thinking, walking, sensing machines that will be at the heart of the robotic revolution.

What this book covers

Chapter 1, Configuring and Programming Raspberry Pi, begins with a discussion on how to connect power, and it continues through setting up a full system that's configured and ready to begin connecting any of the amazing devices and Software capabilities to develop advanced robotics applications.

Chapter 2, Building the Biped, shows how to construct the mechanics of the biped platform whether you want to use 3D print, purchase, or construct your own legs and body.

Chapter 3, Motion for the Biped, talks about how once you have the platform built, you'll need to program it to walk, wave, play dead, or perform any number of neat motion segments so that you can coordinate the movement of your platform.

Chapter 4, Avoiding Obstacles Using Sensors, shows you how to add IR sensors so that you can avoid running into barriers.

Chapter 5, Path Planning and Your Biped, covers how to plan the movement of your biped. As you move around, you'll want to be able to move from point A to point B.

Chapter 6, Adding Vision to Your Biped, provides the details of how to connect a webcam, the hardware, and the software so that we can use it to input visual data into our system.

Chapter 7, Accessing Your Biped Remotely, covers the basics of how to configure the Raspberry Pi as a wireless access point so that you can control your biped remotely.

What you need for this book

Here is the list of what you need:

- Raspbian
- putty
- Image Writer for Windows
- libusb-1.0-0-dev
- VncServer

Who this book is for

This book is for anyone who has some background in using the Raspberry Pi to create robotics projects. Some programming background is assumed as you create a biped robot that can walk, sense its environment, plan its movements, and follow movement and color—all autonomously.

Conventions

In this book, you will find a number of text styles that distinguish between different kinds of information. Here are some examples of these styles and an explanation of their meaning.

Code words in text, database table names, folder names, filenames, file extensions, pathnames, dummy URLs, user input, and Twitter handles are shown as follows: "However, you do need to find the /dev device label for your card"

Any command-line input or output is written as follows:

```
sudo dd if=2015-01-31-raspbian.img  of=/dev/sdX
```

New terms and **important words** are shown in bold. Words that you see on the screen, for example, in menus or dialog boxes, appear in the text like this: "Clicking the **Next** button moves you to the next screen."

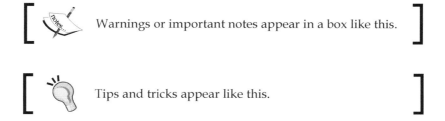

Warnings or important notes appear in a box like this.

Tips and tricks appear like this.

Reader feedback

Feedback from our readers is always welcome. Let us know what you think about this book—what you liked or disliked. Reader feedback is important for us as it helps us develop titles that you will really get the most out of.

To send us general feedback, simply e-mail feedback@packtpub.com, and mention the book's title in the subject of your message.

If there is a topic that you have expertise in and you are interested in either writing or contributing to a book, see our author guide at www.packtpub.com/authors.

Customer support

Now that you are the proud owner of a Packt book, we have a number of things to help you to get the most from your purchase.

Downloading the color images of this book

We also provide you with a PDF file that has color images of the screenshots/ diagrams used in this book. The color images will help you better understand the changes in the output. You can download this file from https://www.packtpub. com/sites/default/files/downloads/Raspberry_Pi_Robotics_Essentials_ Graphics.pdf.

Errata

Although we have taken every care to ensure the accuracy of our content, mistakes do happen. If you find a mistake in one of our books — maybe a mistake in the text or the code — we would be grateful if you could report this to us. By doing so, you can save other readers from frustration and help us improve subsequent versions of this book. If you find any errata, please report them by visiting http://www.packtpub. com/submit-errata, selecting your book, clicking on the **Errata Submission Form** link, and entering the details of your errata. Once your errata are verified, your submission will be accepted and the errata will be uploaded to our website or added to any list of existing errata under the Errata section of that title.

To view the previously submitted errata, go to https://www.packtpub.com/books/ content/support and enter the name of the book in the search field. The required information will appear under the **Errata** section.

Piracy

Piracy of copyrighted material on the Internet is an ongoing problem across all media. At Packt, we take the protection of our copyright and licenses very seriously. If you come across any illegal copies of our works in any form on the Internet, please provide us with the location address or website name immediately so that we can pursue a remedy.

Please contact us at copyright@packtpub.com with a link to the suspected pirated material.

We appreciate your help in protecting our authors and our ability to bring you valuable content.

Questions

If you have a problem with any aspect of this book, you can contact us at questions@packtpub.com, and we will do our best to address the problem.

1
Configuring and Programming Raspberry Pi

Robots are beginning to infiltrate our world. They come in all shapes and sizes, with a wide range of capabilities. And, just like the evolution of the personal computer before them, much of what is happening in the robot development world is coming from hobbyists and do-it-yourselfers that are using a new generation of inexpensive hardware and free, open source software to build machines with all kinds of amazing capabilities. In this book, you will learn how to build robots by building a robot, a four-legged quadruped with sensor and vision capabilities. The skills you will learn, however, can also be used on a wide variety of walking, rolling, swimming, or flying robots.

In this chapter, you'll learn:

- How to configure your Raspberry Pi, the control center of your robot, with the Raspbian operating system
- How to set up a remote development environment so you can program your robot
- Basic programming skills in both Python and C so you can both create and edit the programs your robot will need to do all those amazing things

Configuring Raspberry Pi – the brain of your robot

One of the most important parts of your robot is the processor system you use to control all the different hardware. In this book, you'll learn how to use Raspberry Pi, a small, inexpensive, easy-to-use processor system. Raspberry Pi comes in several flavors – the original A and B model, and the new and improved A+ and B+ model. The B+ flavor is the most popular and comes with additional input/output capability, four USB connections, more memory, and will be the flavor we'll focus on in this book.

Here are the items you'll need to set up an initial Raspberry Pi development environment:

- A Raspberry Pi, Model B 2. There are three other Raspberry Pi models, the B+, the B, and the A. These are models with less processing power and different hardware configurations. In this book, we'll focus on the Raspberry Pi Model B 2; it has the best processing power and the most useful input/output access. However, many of the items in this book will also work with the Raspberry Pi B+ and A versions, perhaps with some additional hardware.

- The USB cable to provide power to the board.

- A microSD card — at least 4 GB.

- A microSD card writer.

- Another computer that is connected to the Internet.

- An Internet connection for the board — for the initial configuration steps, you'll need a LAN cable and wired LAN connection.

- A wireless LAN device.

Here is what the Raspberry Pi B 2 board looks like:

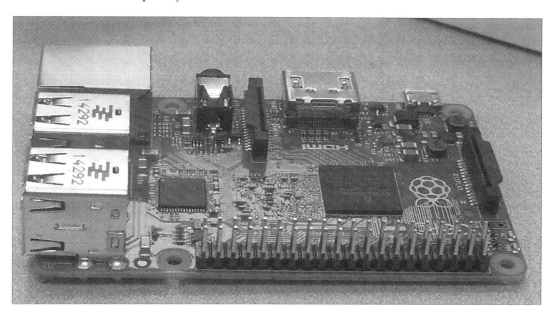

You should also acquaint yourself with the different connections on the board. Here they are on the B 2, labelled for your information:

Installing the operating system

Before you get started, you'll need to download and create a card with the Raspbian operating system. You are going to install Raspbian, an open source version of the Debian version of Linux, on your Raspberry Pi.

There are two approaches to getting Raspbian on your board. The board is getting popular enough that you can now buy an SD card that already has Rasbpian installed, or you can download it onto your personal computer and then install it on the card. If you are going to download a distribution, you need to decide if you are going to use a Windows computer to download and create an SD card, or a Linux machine.

No matter which machine you are going to use, you'll need to download an image. Open a browser window. Go to the Raspberry Pi site, www.raspberrypi.org, and select **Downloads** from the top of the page. This will give you a variety of download choices. Go to the **Raspbian** section and select the .zip file just to the right of the image identifier. This will download an archived file that has the image for your Raspbian operating system. Note the default username and password; you'll need those later.

If you're using Windows, you'll need to unzip the file using an archiving program like 7-Zip. This will leave you with a file that has the .img extension, a file that can be imaged on your card. Next, you'll need a program that can write the image to the card. Use Image Writer if you are going to create your card using a Windows machine. You can find a link to this program at the top of the download section on the www.raspberrypi.org website. Plug your card into the PC, run this program, and you should see this:

Select the correct card and image; it should look something like this:

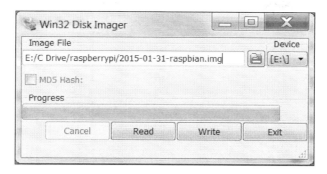

Then select **Write**. This will take some time, but when it is complete, eject the card from the PC.

If you are using Linux, you'll need to unarchive the file and then write it to the card. You can do all of this with one command. However, you do need to find the `/dev` device label for your card. You can do this with the `ls -la /dev/sd*` command. If you run this before you plug in your card, you might see something like the following:

```
richard@vicki-automated: ~
richard@vicki-automated:~$ ls -la /dev/sd*
brw-rw---- 1 root disk 8, 0 Jul  4 10:34 /dev/sda
brw-rw---- 1 root disk 8, 1 Jul  4 10:34 /dev/sda1
brw-rw---- 1 root disk 8, 2 Jul  4 10:34 /dev/sda2
brw-rw---- 1 root disk 8, 5 Jul  4 10:34 /dev/sda5
richard@vicki-automated:~$
```

After plugging in your card, you might see something like the following:

```
🗙 ⊝ ⊝    richard@vicki-automated: ~
richard@vicki-automated:~$ ls -la /dev/sd*
brw-rw---- 1 root disk 8,  0 Jul  4 10:34 /dev/sda
brw-rw---- 1 root disk 8,  1 Jul  4 10:34 /dev/sda1
brw-rw---- 1 root disk 8,  2 Jul  4 10:34 /dev/sda2
brw-rw---- 1 root disk 8,  5 Jul  4 10:34 /dev/sda5
brw-rw---- 1 root disk 8, 16 Jul 11 09:50 /dev/sdb
brw-rw---- 1 root disk 8, 17 Jul 11 09:50 /dev/sdb1
brw-rw---- 1 root disk 8, 18 Jul 11 09:50 /dev/sdb2
richard@vicki-automated:~$ █
```

Note that your card is `sdb`. Now, go to the directory where you downloaded the archived image file and issue the following command:

```
sudo dd if=2015-01-31-raspbian.img  of=/dev/sdX
```

The `2015-01-31-raspbian.img` command will be replaced with the image file that you downloaded, and `/dev/sdX` will be replaced with your card ID; in this example, `/dev/sdb`.

Once your card image has been created, install it on the Raspberry Pi. You'll also need to plug your Raspberry Pi into the LAN cable, and the LAN cable into your wired LAN network.

 If you don't have a wired connection, you can complete the following steps by connecting your Raspberry Pi directly to a monitor, keyboard, and mouse.

Power the device. The **POWER LED** should light and your device should boot from the card. To configure the card, you'll need to access it remotely. To do this, you'll now need to connect to the device via SSH, a secure protocol that allows you to control one computer remotely from another computer.

One of the challenges of accessing the system remotely is that you need to know the IP address of your board. There is a way to discover this by using an IP scanner application. There are several scanners available for free; on Windows, a possible choice is Advanced IP Scanner, which is available from `http://www.advanced-ip-scanner.com/`. Here is what the program looks like when it is run:

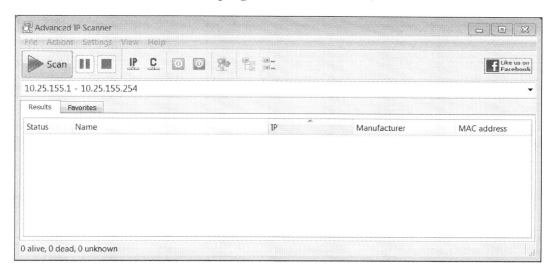

Clicking on the **Scan** selector scans for all the devices connected to the network. You can also do this in Linux; one application for IP scanning in Linux is called Nmap. To install Nmap, type in `sudo apt-get install nmap`. To run Nmap, type in `sudo nmap -sP 10.25.155.1/154` and the scanner will scan the addresses from 10.25.155.1 to 10.25.155.154.

These scanners can let you know which addresses are being used, and this should then let you find your Raspberry Pi IP address. Since you are going to access your device via SSH, you'll also need an SSH terminal program running on your remote computer. If you are running Microsoft Windows, you can download such an application. One simple and easy choice is Putty. It is free and does a very good job of allowing you to save your configuration so you don't have to type it in each time. This program is available at `www.putty.org`.

Download Putty on your Microsoft Windows machine. Then run `putty.exe`. You should see a configuration window. It will look something like the following screenshot:

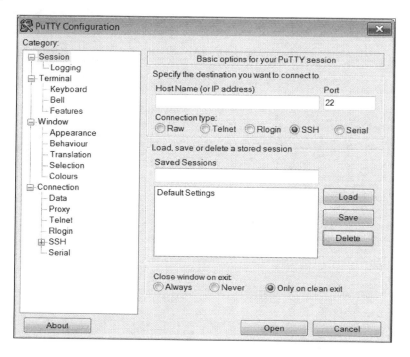

Type in the `inet addr` from the IP Scanner in the **Host Name** space and make sure that the SSH is selected. You may want to save this configuration under Raspberry Pi so you can reload it each time.

When you click on **Open**, the system will try to open a terminal window onto your Raspberry Pi via the LAN connection. The first time you do this, you will get a warning about an RSA key, as the two computers don't know about each other; so Windows is complaining that a computer it doesn't know is about to be connected in a fairly intimate way. Simply click on **OK**, and you should get a terminal with a login prompt, like the following screenshot:

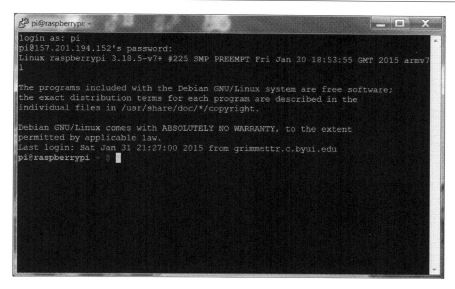

Now you can log in and issue commands to your Raspberry Pi. If you'd like to do this from a Linux machine, the process is even simpler. Bring up a terminal window and then type in `ssh pi@xxx.xxx.xxx.xxx -p 22`, where `xxx.xxx.xxx.xxx` is the `inet addr` of your device. This will then bring you to the login screen of your Raspberry Pi, which should look similar to the previous screenshot.

After your log in, you should get a screen that looks like the following:

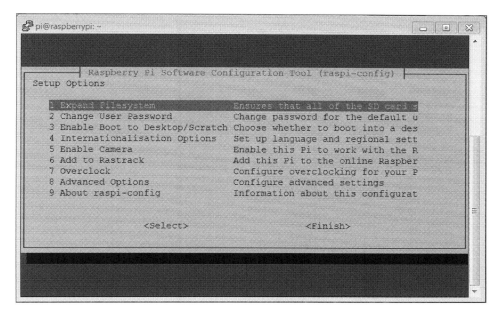

First, you'll want to expand the file system to take up the entire card. So, hit the *Enter* key, and you'll see the following screen:

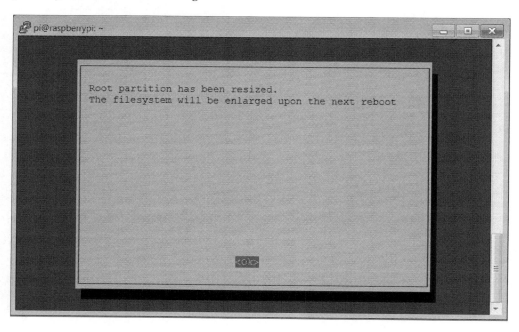

Hit *Enter* once again and you'll go back to the main configuration screen. Now, select the **Enable Boot to Desktop/Scratch** option.

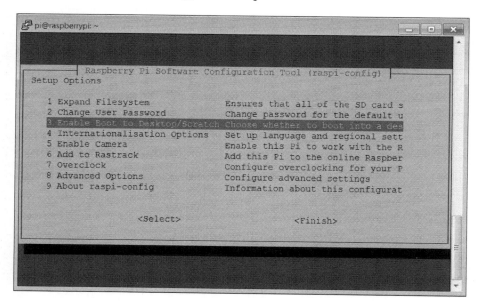

When you hit *Enter*, you'll see the following screen:

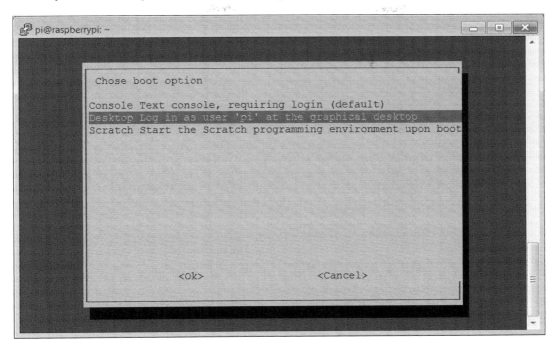

You can also choose to overclock your device. This is a way for you to get higher performance from your system. However, there is a risk that you can end up with a system that has reliability problems.

Once you are done and are back at the main configuration menu, hit the *Tab* key until you are positioned over the **<Finish>** selection, then hit *Enter*. Then, hit *Enter* again so that you can reboot your Raspberry Pi. This time, when you log in, you will not see any configuration selections. However, if you ever want to change your configuration choices, you can run the configuration tool by typing in `raspi-config` at the command prompt.

Adding a remote graphical user interface

For some steps in your robot build, you will need a graphical look at your system. You can get this on your Raspberry Pi using an application called vncserver. You'll need to install a version of this on your Raspberry Pi by typing in `sudo apt-get install tightvncserver` in a terminal window on your Raspberry Pi.

Tightvncserver is an application that will allow you to remotely view your complete graphical desktop. Once you have it installed, you can do the following:

1. You'll need to start the server by typing in `vncserver` in a terminal window on the Raspberry Pi.

2. You will then be prompted for a password, prompted to verify the password, and then asked if you'd like to have a view only password. Remember the password you entered; you'll need it to remotely log in via a VNC viewer.

3. You'll need a VNC viewer application for your remote computer; a good choice is Real VNC, available from `http://www.realvnc.com/download/viewer/`. When you run it, you should see this:

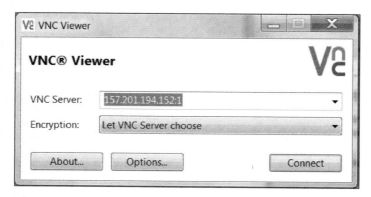

4. Enter the VNC server address, which is the IP address of your Raspberry Pi, and click on **Connect**. You will get a warning about an unencrypted connection; select **Continue** and you will get this pop-up window:

5. Type in the password you just entered while starting the vncserver, and you should then get a graphical view of your Raspberry Pi, which looks like the following screenshot:

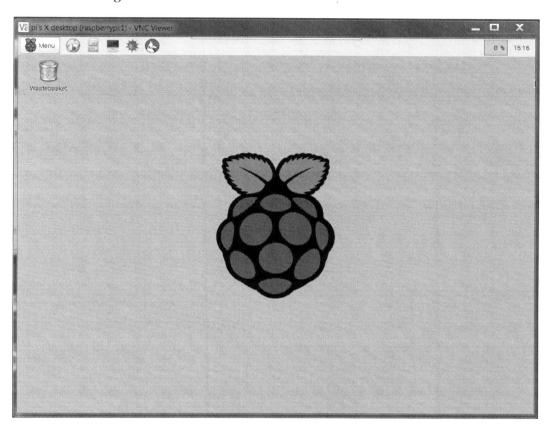

You can now access all the capabilities of your system, albeit they may be slower if you are doing a graphics-intense data transfer. To avoid having to type in vncserver each time you boot your Raspberry Pi, use the instructions at http://www. havetheknowhow.com/Configure-the-server/Run-VNC-on-boot.html.

Vncserver is also available via Linux. You can use an application called Remote Desktop Viewer to view the remote Raspberry Pi Windows system. If you have not installed this application, install it using the updated software application based on the type of Linux system you have. Once you have the software, do the following:

1. Run the application, and you should see the following screenshot:

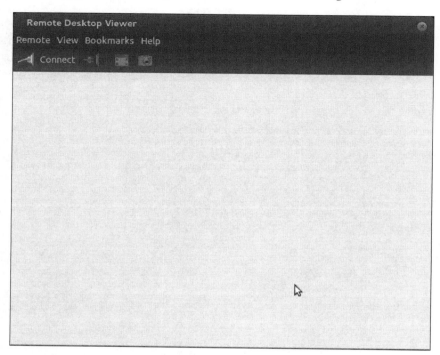

2. Make sure that vncserver is running on the Raspberry Pi; the easiest way to do this is to log in using SSH and run vncserver at the prompt. Now, click on **Connect** on the **Remote Desktop Viewer**. Fill in the screen as follows. Under the **Protocol** selection, choose **VNC**, and you should see the following screenshot:

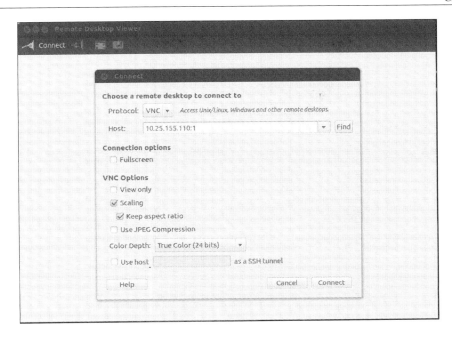

3. Now, enter the Host inet address—make sure to include :1 at the end, and then click on **Connect**. You'll need to enter the vncserver password you set up, like the following screenshot:

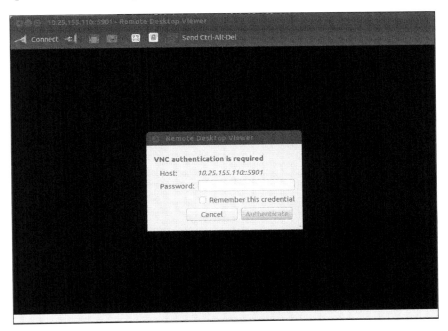

You should now see the graphical screen of the Raspberry Pi. You are ready to start interacting with the system!

Establishing wireless access

Now that your system is configured, the next step is to connect your Raspberry Pi to your remote computer using wireless. To do this, you'll add a wireless USB device and configure it. See `http://elinux.org/RPi_USB_Wi-Fi_Adapters` to identify wireless devices that have been verified to work with Raspberry Pi. Here is one available at many online electronics outlets:

To connect to your wireless LAN, boot the system and edit the network file by typing in `sudo nano /etc/network/interfaces`. Then, edit the file to look like this:

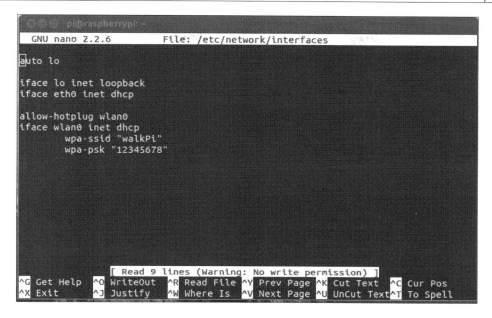

```
  GNU nano 2.2.6          File: /etc/network/interfaces

auto lo

iface lo inet loopback
iface eth0 inet dhcp

allow-hotplug wlan0
iface wlan0 inet dhcp
        wpa-ssid "walkPi"
        wpa-psk "12345678"




                  [ Read 9 lines (Warning: No write permission) ]
^G Get Help  ^O WriteOut  ^R Read File ^Y Prev Page ^K Cut Text  ^C Cur Pos
^X Exit      ^J Justify   ^W Where Is  ^V Next Page ^U UnCut Text^T To Spell
```

Reboot your device and it should now be connected to your wireless network.

If you are using a US keyboard, you may need to edit the keyboard file for your keyboard to use nano effectively. To do this, type in sudo nano /etc/default/keyboard and change XKBLAYOUT="gb" to XKBLAYOUT="us".

Your system has lots of capabilities. Feel free to play with the system, which will give you an understanding of what is already there and what you'll want to add from a software perspective.

Programming on Raspberry Pi

One last bit of introduction. You'll need some basic programming skills to be successful on your project. This section will touch a little on Python and C programming on the Raspberry Pi.

Creating and running Python programs on the Raspberry Pi

You'll be using Python for two reasons. First, it is a simple language that is intuitive and very easy to use. Second, a lot of open source functionality in the robotics world is available in Python. To work the examples in this section, you'll need a version of Python installed. Fortunately, the basic Raspbian system has a version already installed, so you are ready to begin.

> If you are new to programming, there are a number of different websites that provide interactive tutorials. If you'd like to practice some of the basic programming concepts in Python using these tools, go to www.codeacademy.com or http://www.learnpython.org/ and give it a try.

But, to get you started, let's first cover how to create and run a Python file. It turns out that Python is an interactive language, so you could run Python and then type in commands one at a time. However, you want to use Python to create programs, so you are going to create Python programs and then run these programs from the command line by invoking Python.

Open an example Python file by typing in emacs example.py. Now, put some code in the file. Start with the lines shown in the following screenshot:

```
pi@raspberrypi: ~
File Edit Options Buffers Tools Python Help
a = input("Input value: ")
b = input("Input second value: ")
c = a + b
print c
```

Your code may be color coded. I have removed the color coding here so that it is easier to read.

Let's go through the code to see what is happening:

1. `a = input("Input value: ")`: One of the basic needs of a program is to get input from the user. The `raw_input` part allows us to do that. The data will be input by the user and stored in a. The prompt `"Input value:"` will be shown to the user.

2. `b = input("Input second value: ")`: This data will also be input by the user and stored in b. The prompt `"Input second value:"` will be shown to the user.

3. `c = a + b`: This is an example of something you can do with the data; in this example, you can add a and b.

4. `print c`: Another basic need of our program is to print out results. The print command prints out the value of c.

Once you have created your program, save it (using `ctrl-x ctrl-s`) and quit emacs (using `ctrl-x ctrl-c`). Now, from the command line, run your program by typing in `python example.py`. You should see something similar to the following screenshot:

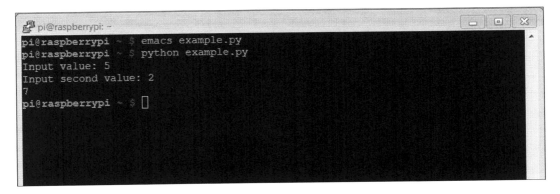

You can also run the program right from the command line without typing in `python example.py` by adding one line to the program. Now, the program should look like the following screenshot:

Adding `#!/usr/bin/python` as the first line simply makes this file available for us to execute from the command line. Once you have saved the file and exited emacs, type in `chmod +x example.py`. This will change the file's execution permissions, so the computer will now believe it and execute it. You should be able to simply type in `./example.py` and the program should run, as shown in the following screenshot:

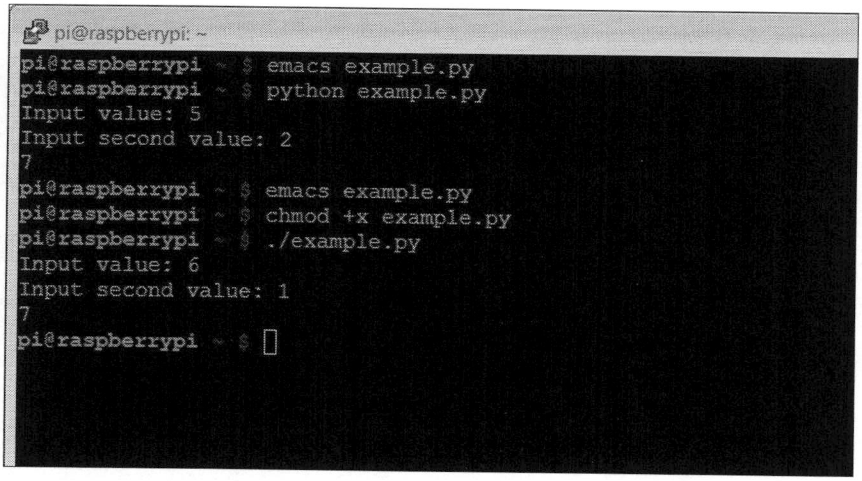

Note that if you simply type in `example.py`, the system will not find the executable file. In this case, the file has not been registered with the system, so you have to give it a path to the file. In this case, `./` is the current directory.

An introduction to the C/C++ programming language

Now that you've been introduced to a simple programming language in Python, you'll also need a bit of exposure to a more complex, but powerful, language called C. C is the original language of Linux and has been around for many decades, but is still widely used by open source developers. It is similar to Python, but is also a bit different, and since you may need to understand and make changes to C code, you should be familiar with it and know how it is used.

As with Python, you will need to have access to the language capabilities. These come in the form of a compiler and build system, which turns your text files into ones that contain programs to machine code that the processor can actually execute. To do this, type in `sudo apt-get install build-essential`. This will install the programs you need to turn your code into executables for the system.

Now that the tools are installed, let's walk through some simple examples. Here is the first C/C++ code example:

```cpp
#include <iostream>

int main()
{
  int a;
  int b;
  int c;

  std::cout << "Input value: ";
  std::cin >> a;
  std::cout << "Input second value: ";
  std::cin >> b;

  c = a + b;

  std::cout << c << std::endl;

  return 0;
}
```

```
-UU-:----F1   example2.cpp   All L13   (C++/l Abbrev)--------------
Wrote /home/pi/example2.cpp
```

The following is an explanation of the code:

- `#include <iostream>`: This is a library that is included so that your program can input data from the keyboard and output information to the screen.

- `int main()`: As with Python, we can put functions and classes in the file, but you will always want to start execution at a known point; C defines this as the `main` function.

- `int a;`: This defines a variable named a, of type `int`. C is what we call a strongly typed language, which means that we need to declare the type of the variable we are defining. The normal types are `int`, a number that has no decimal points; `float`, a number that requires decimal points; `char`, a character of text, and `bool`, a `true` or `false` value. Also note that every line in C ends with the `;` character.

- `int b;`: This defines a variable named b, of type `int`.

- `int c;`: This defines a variable named c, of type `int`.

- `std::cout << "Input value: ";`: This will display the string `"Input value: "` on the screen.

- `std::cin >> a;`: The input that the user types will go into the variable a.

- `std::cout << "Input second value: ";`: This will display the string `"Input second value: "` on the screen.

- `std::cin >> b;`: The input that the user types will go into the variable b.

- `c = a + b`: The statement is a simple addition of two values.

- `std::cout << c << std::endl;`: The `cout` command prints out the value of c. The `endl` command at the end prints out a carriage return so that the next character appears on the next line.

- `return 0;`: The main function ends and returns `0`.

To run this program, you'll need to run a compile process to turn it into an executable program that you can run. To do this, after you have created the program, type in `g++ example2.cpp -o example2`. This will then process your program, turning it into a file that the computer can execute. The name of the executable program will be `example2` (as specified by the name after the `-o` option).

If you run an `ls` on your directory after you have compiled this, you should see the `example2` file in your directory, as shown in the following screenshot:

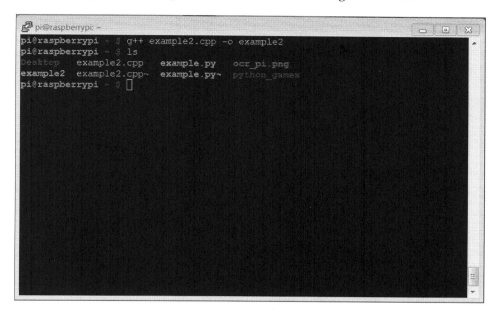

If you run into a problem, the compiler will try to help you figure out the problem. If, for example, you forgot the `int` before `a` in the expression `int a`, you would get the following error when you try to compile:

The error message indicates a problem in the `int main()` function and tells you that the variable `a` was not successfully declared. Once you have the file compiled, to run the executable, type in `./example2`, and you should be able to create the following result:

```
pi@raspberrypi: ~
pi@raspberrypi ~ $ emacs example2.cpp
pi@raspberrypi ~ $ g++ example2.cpp -o example2
example2.cpp: In function 'int main()':
example2.cpp:6:3: error: 'a' was not declared in this scope
pi@raspberrypi ~ $ emacs example2.cpp
pi@raspberrypi ~ $ g++ example2.cpp -o example2
pi@raspberrypi ~ $ ./example2
Input value: 9
Input second value: 2
11
pi@raspberrypi ~ $ []
```

If you are interested in learning more about C programming, there are several good tutorials out on the Internet that can help-for example, at `http://www.cprogramming.com/tutorial/c-tutorial.html` and `http://thenewboston.org/list.php?cat=14`.

There is one more aspect of C you will need to know about. The compile process that you just encountered seemed fairly straightforward. However, if you have your functionality distributed between a lot of files or need lots of libraries, the command-line approach to executing a compile can get unwieldy.

The C development environment provides a way to automate this process; it is called the make process. When using this, you create a text program named `makefile` that defines the files you want to include and compile, and then, instead of typing a long command or set of commands, you simply type in `make` and the system will execute a compile based on the definitions in the `makefile` program. There are several good tutorials that talk more about this system-for example, `http://www.cs.colby.edu/maxwell/courses/tutorials/maketutor/` or `http://mrbook.org/tutorials/make/`.

Now you are equipped to edit and create your own programming files. The next chapters will provide you with lots of opportunities to practice your skills as you translate lines of code into cool robotic capabilities.

Summary

Congratulations! You have your Raspberry Pi up and working. No gathering dust in the bin for this piece of hardware, Now, you are ready to start commanding your Raspberry Pi to do something.

The next chapter will show you how to construct your biped robot.

2
Building the Biped

Now that you've got your Raspberry Pi 2 Model B all configured and ready to go, you'll need to add some hardware to control and interface. In this chapter, you'll learn:

- How to build a basic 10 **Degrees of Freedom** (**DOF**) biped
- How to use a servo motor controller connected to the USB port of the Raspberry Pi to control the servos to make your robot move

Building robots that can walk

There are several choices when considering how to create a mobile robot. One of the more interesting choices is a robot that can walk. This normally comes in three versions: a biped robot with two legs, a biped robot with four legs, and a hexapod robot with six legs. While each offers an interesting and different set of possibilities, in this chapter, you'll build a basic, 10 DOF biped.

You'll be using a total of 10 servos for your project, as each leg has 5 points that can move, or 5 degrees of freedom (DOF). As servos are the most critical component of this project, it is perhaps useful to go through a tutorial on servos and learn how to control them.

How servo motors work

Servo motors are somewhat similar to DC motors. However, there is an important difference. While DC motors are generally designed to move in a continuous way—rotating 360 degrees at a given speed—servos are generally designed to move to a limited set of angles. In other words, in the DC motor world, you generally want your motors to spin with a continuous rotation speed that you control. In the servo world, you want your motor to move to a specific position that you control.

This is done by sending a **Pulse-Width-Modulated (PWM)** signal to the control connector of the servo. The length of this pulse will control the angle of the servo like this:

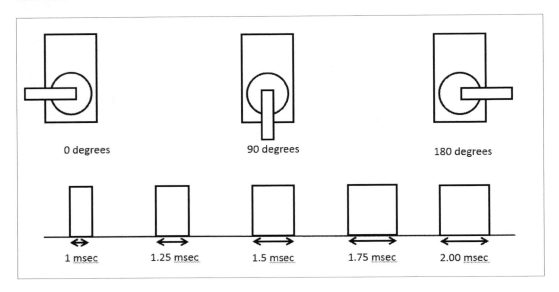

These pulses are sent out with a repetition rate of 60 Hz. You can position the servo to any angle by setting the correct control pulse.

Building the biped platform

There are several approaches to building your biped platform. Perhaps the most simple is to purchase a set of basic parts; this is the example you'll see in this chapter. There are several kit possibilities out there, including one at http:// www.robotshop.com/en/lynxmotion-biped-robot-scout-bps-ns-servos. html, a kit like the one offered at http://www.ebay.com/itm/10-DOF-Biped-Robot-Mechanical-Leg-Robot-Servo-Motor-Bracket-NO-Servo-Motor-good-/131162548695?pt=LH_DefaultDomain_0&hash=item1e89e5a9d7, or the one at http://www.amazon.com/gp/product/B00DR7GA4I/ref=oh_aui_detailpage_o04_s00?ie=UTF8&psc=1. This is the specific kit we'll use in this chapter.

In the end, your biped will work more like the legs of a Tyrannosaurus Rex of a human, but this will make it easier to program, and it will power down more gracefully. It will also be a bit more stable.

You'll also need 10 standard size servos. There are several possible choices, but **Hitec** servos are relatively inexpensive servos and you can get them at most hobby shops and online electronics retailers. One of the important steps in this process is to select the model of the servo. Servos come in different model numbers, primarily based on the amount of torque they can generate.

Torque is the force that the servo can exert to move the part connected to it. In this case, your servos will need to lift and move the weight associated with your biped, so you'll need a servo with enough torque to do this. However, there are different torque needs for your biped robot. The angle joints will not lift the entire leg, so they can be servos with a lower servo rating, for example, the HS-422 servos. For the knee servo, you'll need a more powerful servo. In this case, I suggest that you use model HS-645MGHB servos. The hip joint that lifts the leg is where you will need the most torque to be able to lift the leg. Here, too, I suggest that you use the model HS-645MG servos. You can also just use 10 HS-645MG servos for all the servos, but they are more expensive, so using different servos will save you some money.

One final piece that you'll need is some metal servo horns. These servo horns are optional, but they will make your biped robot much more solid than the plastic servo horns that normally come with the servos. Here is a picture of one of these horns:

Here are the steps to assemble the biped:

1. Attach the first ankle servo to the foot. To do this, find the foot plate, as shown here:

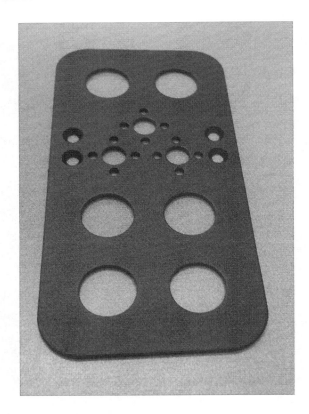

This is the bottom of the foot. Notice the beveled holes-you'll be using bevel-headed bolts to connect a servo bracket to the foot plate, as shown here:

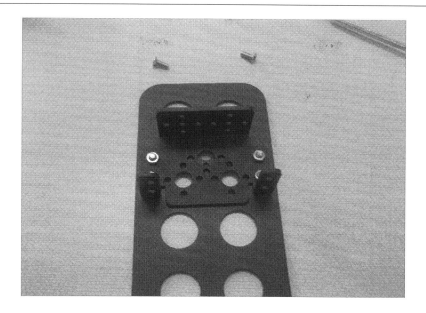

2. Make sure that the bottom of the foot is flat. Before you mount the servo to this bracket, you'll first connect a U-shaped bracket to this servo bracket using one of the bearings in the kit, like this:

3. Finally, mount one of the servos in the bracket and connect the U-shaped bracket to the servo horn, as shown here:

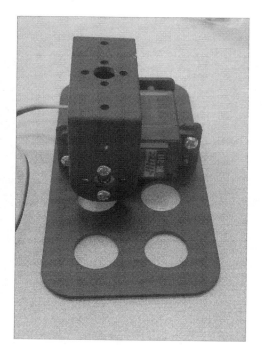

4. This first servo should allow your biped to move the foot, tipping it side to side. Now, add the second ankle servo to the foot. This will allow your biped to tip the ankle front to back. To do this, connect a servo bracket to the assembly you just created, and then add a U bracket to this assembly, like this:

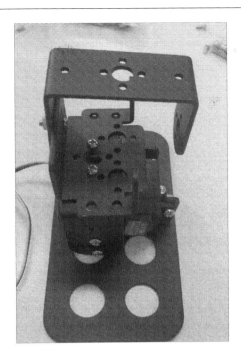

5. Now, add the bracket to this assembly, like this:

6. Now, you can add the knee servo to your biped. However, you'll first want to connect the upper leg, the longest U bracket, to a servo bracket, like this:

7. Now, connect this assembly, using another bearing, to the lower leg that you have already built, like this:

8. Now, you can mount the knee servo in this place. If you have different servos, use a more powerful servo in the knee joint. Here is a picture:

9. The last step is to put the hip together. First, you'll put the servo that turns the leg, connecting it to a servo bracket, as shown here:

10. Now, connect this servo bracket to the long U bracket, and mount the servo that lifts the entire leg. This is another place; if you are using different servos, you'll want to use a servo with a significant torque. The entire assembly should look like this:

11. Put the other leg together. It will be a mirror image of the first leg.

12. Now, you'll connect both legs to the hip by first connecting a servo bracket connector to the hip piece, in two places, like this:

13. Finally, mount the top of the leg servos into the brackets, like this:

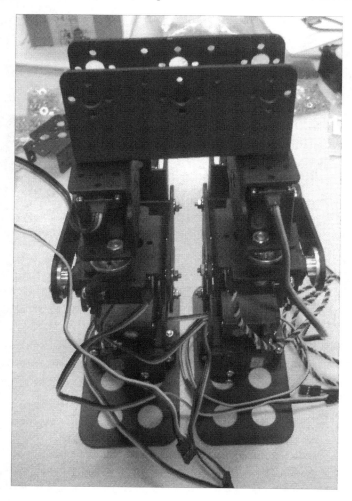

Your biped is now ready to walk. Now that you have the basic hardware assembled, you can turn your attention to the electronics.

Using a servo controller to control the servos

To make your biped walk, you first need to connect the servo motor controller to the servos. The servo controller you are going to use for this project is a simple servo motor controller utilizing the USB from Pololu—Pololu item number 1354 is available at pololu.com—that can control 18 servo motors. Here is a picture of the unit:

Make sure that you order the assembled version. This piece of hardware will turn USB commands from Raspberry Pi into signals that control your servo motors. Pololu creates a number of different versions of this controller, and each one is able to control a certain number of servos. In this case, you may want to choose the 18 servo version, so that you can control all 12 servos with one controller, and you may also add an additional servo to control the direction of a camera or sensor. You could also choose the 12 servo version. One advantage of the 18 servo controller is the ease of connecting power to the unit via screw-type connectors.

There are two connections you'll need to make to the servo controller in order to get started: the first to the servo motors and the second to a battery.

First, connect the servos to the controller. In order to be consistent, let's connect your 12 servos to the connections marked 0 through 11 on the controller using this configuration:

Servo Connector	Servo
0	Right ankle in/out
1	Right ankle front/back
2	Right knee
3	Right hip up/down
4	Right hip turn
5	Left ankle in/out
6	Left ankle front/back
7	Left knee
8	Left up/down
9	Left hip turn

Here is a picture of the back of the controller; this will tell us where to connect our servos:

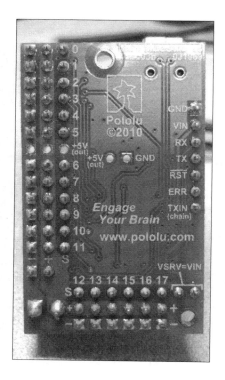

Now, you need to connect the servo motor controller to your battery. For this project, you can use a 2S RC LiPo battery; it will supply the 7.4 volts and the current required by your servos, which can be on the order of 2 amps. Here is a picture:

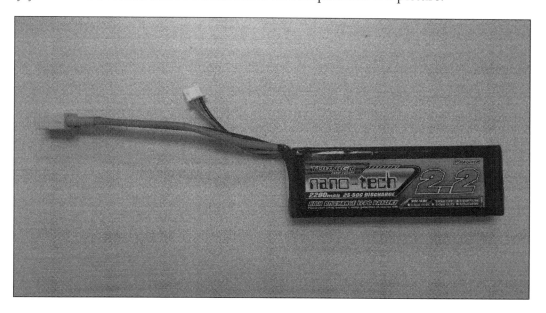

This battery will come with two connectors, one with larger gauge wires for normal usage and a smaller connector to connect to the battery recharger. You can use the XT60 Connector Pairs, solder some wires to the mating connector of the battery, and then insert the bare end of the wires into the servo controller.

Your system is now functional. You can connect the motor controller to your personal computer to check whether you can communicate with it. To do this, connect a mini USB cable between the servo controller and your personal computer.

Communicating with the servo controller with a PC

Now that the hardware is connected, you can use some software provided by Polulu to control the servos. Let's do this using your personal computer. First, download the Polulu SW from www.pololu.com/docs/0J40/3.a, and install it based on the instructions on the website. Once it is installed, run the software, and you should see this screen:

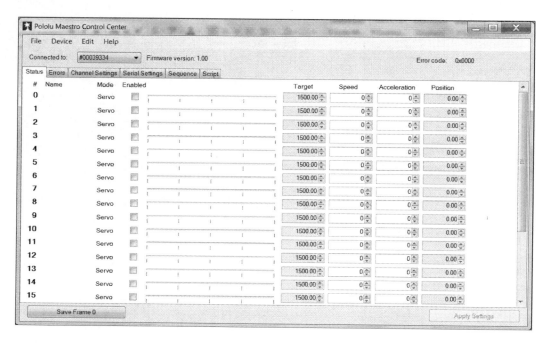

First, you will need to change the configuration in Serial Settings, so select the **Serial Settings** tabs, and you should see this:

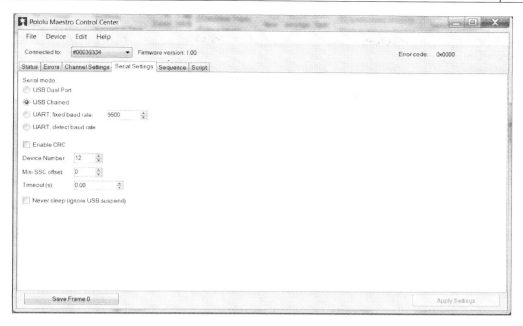

Make sure that USB Chained is selected; this will allow you to connect and control the motor controller over USB. Now, go back to the main screen by selecting the **Status** tab; now, you can actually turn on the 10 servos. The screen should look like this:

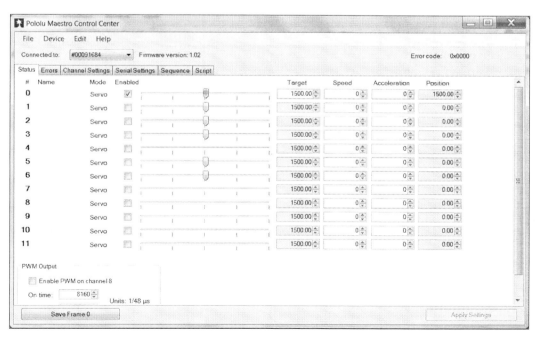

Now you can use the sliders to actually control the servos. Turn on servo 0. Make sure that servo 0 moves the lower-right ankle servo. You can also use this to center the servos. Set servo 1 so that the slider is in the middle. Now, unscrew the servo horn on the servo until the servos are centered at this location. At the zero location of all servos, your biped should look like this:

Connecting the servo controller to the Raspberry Pi

You've checked the servo motor controller and the servos. You can now connect the motor controller up to the Raspberry Pi and make sure that you can control the servos from it.

Now, let's talk to the motor controller. Here are the steps:

1. Connect Raspberry Pi to the motor controller by connecting a mini USB to a mini USB cable. Connect the cable to the USB host connection on the Raspberry Pi, like this:

2. Download the Linux code from Pololu at www.pololu.com/docs/0J40/3.b. Perhaps the best way to do this is to log on to your Raspberry Pi and then type wget http://www.pololu.com/file/download/maestro-linux-100507.tar.gz?file_id=0J315.

3. Then, move the file using mv maestro-linux-100507.tar.gz\?file_id\=0J315 maestro-linux-100507.tar.gz.

4. Unpack the file by typing `tar -xvf maestro_linux_011507.tar.gz`. This will create a directory called `maestro_linux`. Go to this directory by typing `cd maestro_linux`, and then type `ls`; you should see something like this:

The `README.txt` document will give you explicit instructions on how to install the software. Unfortunately, you can't run **MaestroControlCenter** on your Raspberry Pi; the version of Windows it uses doesn't support the graphics, but you can control your servos using the **UscCmd** command-line application. First, type `./UscCmd --list`, and you should see the following:

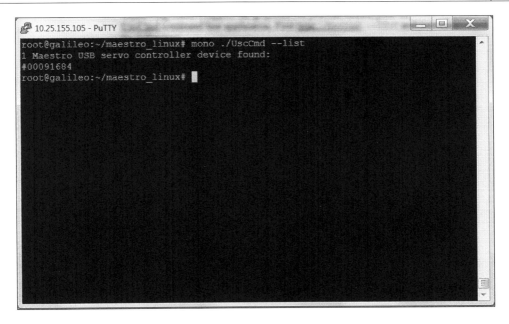

The unit sees your servo controller. If you just type ./UscCmd, you can see all the commands you could send to your controller:

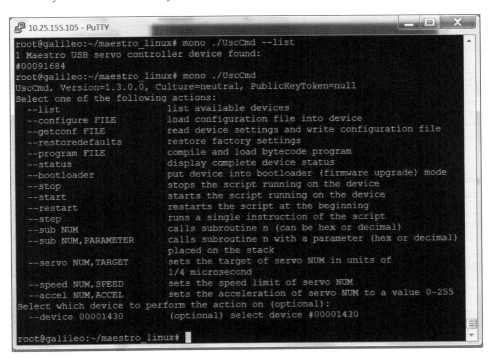

Note that you can send a specific target angle to a servo, although the target is not in angle values, so it makes it a bit difficult to know where you are sending your servo. With a servo and battery connected to the servo controller, try to type `./UscCmd --servo 0, 10`. The servo will move to its full angle position. Type `./UscCmd -servo 0, 0`, and it will stop the servo from trying to move. In the next section, you'll write some Python code that will translate your angles to the commands that the servo controller will want to see in order to move it to specific angle locations. If you are struggling with the USB connection, refer to `http://www.linux-usb.org/FAQ.html` for more information.

 If you didn't run the Windows version of Maestro Controller and set **Serial Settings** to **USB Chained**, your motor controller may not respond. Rerun the MaestroController code and set **Serial Settings** to **USB Chained**.

Creating a program to control your biped

Now you know that you can talk to your servo motor controller and move your servos. In this section, you'll create a Python program that will let you talk to your servos to move them at specific angles. You can use Python as it is very simple and easy to run.

Let's start with a simple program that will make your legged mobile robot's servos go to 90 degrees (which should be somewhere close to the middle between the 0 to 180 degrees you can set). Here is the code:

```
pi@raspberrypi: ~/maestro-linux
File Edit Options Buffers Tools Python Help
#!/usr/bin/python
import serial
import time

def setAngle(ser, channel, angle):
    minAngle = 0.0
    maxAngle = 180.0
    minTarget = 256.0
    maxTarget = 13120.0
    scaledValue = int((angle / ((maxAngle - minAngle) / (maxTarget - minTarget)\
)) + minTarget)
    commandByte = chr(0x84)
    channelByte = chr(channel)
    lowTargetByte = chr(scaledValue & 0x7F)
    highTargetByte = chr((scaledValue >> 7) & 0x7F)
    command = commandByte + channelByte + lowTargetByte + highTargetByte
    ser.write(command)
    ser.flush()

ser = serial.Serial("/dev/ttyACM0", 9600)

# Home position

for i in range(0, 9):
    setAngle(ser, i ,90)

ser.close()



-UU-:----F1   robot.py        All L1      (Python)-------------------------
For information about GNU Emacs and the GNU system, type C-h C-a.
```

Here is an explanation of the code:

- `#!/usr/bin/python`: This first line allows you to make this Python file execute from the command line.

- `import serial`: This line imports the serial library. You need the serial library to talk to your unit via the USB.

- `def setAngle(ser, channel, angle)`:: This function converts your desired setting of servo and angle into the serial command that the servo motor controller needs. To understand the specifics of the code used to control the servos, refer to `https://www.pololu.com/docs/0J40`.

- `ser = serial.Serial("/dev/ttyACM0", 9600)`: This opens the serial port connection to your servo controller.
- `for i in range(0, 9)`: For loop to access all nine servos.
- `setAngle(ser, i, 90)`: Now, you can set each servo to the middle (home) position. The default would be to set each servo to 90 degrees. If your legs aren't in their middle position, you can adjust them by adjusting the position of the servo horns on each servo.

To access the serial port, you'll need to make sure that you have the Python serial library. If you don't, then type `apt-get install python-serial`. After you have installed the serial library, you can run your program by typing `python quad.py`.

Once you have the basic home position set, you can ask your robot to do something. Let's start by having your biped move its foot. Here is the Python code:

```
#!/usr/bin/python
import serial
import time

def setAngle(ser, channel, angle):
    minAngle = 0.0
    maxAngle = 180.0
    minTarget = 256.0
    maxTarget = 13120.0
    scaledValue = int((angle / ((maxAngle - minAngle) / (maxTarget - minTarget)\
)) + minTarget)
    commandByte = chr(0x84)
    channelByte = chr(channel)
    lowTargetByte = chr(scaledValue & 0x7F)
    highTargetByte = chr((scaledValue >> 7) & 0x7F)
    command = commandByte + channelByte + lowTargetByte + highTargetByte
    ser.write(command)
    ser.flush()

ser = serial.Serial("/dev/ttyACM0", 9600)

# Home position

for i in range(0, 9):
    setAngle(ser, i ,90)

setAngle(ser, 0, 100)
time.sleep(1)
setAngle(ser, 0, 80)
time.sleep(1)
setAngle(ser, 0, 90)
ser.close()
```

In this case, you are using your `setAngle` command to set your servos to manipulate your robot's right ankle.

Summary

You now have a robot than can move! In the next chapter, you'll learn how to make your robot do many amazing things. You'll learn how to make it walk forward and backward and how to make it dance and turn. With some basic knowledge, any number of movements is possible.

3
Motion for the Biped

Now that you've got your biped all up and running, you can start developing interesting ways to make it move. In this chapter, you'll learn

- How to adjust the positions of your servos for the Tyrannosaurus Rex pose
- The basic walking gait for your robot
- The basic turn for your robot

Before you begin, however, it will be best if you create a harness for your biped. Your robot is going to be inherently unstable with only two legs, and, as you experiment, you're going to make some mistakes. With only two legs, these mistakes can, and probably will, result in your robot toppling over, which can damage the robot.

If you have an electronics board vise, or an "Extra Hands" device, they can be useful for this purpose. Here is a picture of how to use this device to create a harness:

If you don't, you can easily create this sort of overhead support using a PVC pipe or wood. Really, just something to keep your biped from crashing over during your experimentation.

A basic stable pose

Now that your biped is built and you know how to program the servos using Python, you can experiment with some basic poses. You'll first create a program that allows you to set individual servos so that you can experiment. Here is the program:

```
pi@raspberrypi: ~/maestro-linux

File Edit Options Buffers Tools Help
#!/usr/bin/python
import serial
import time

def setAngle(ser, channel, angle):
    minAngle = 0.0
    maxAngle = 180.0
    minTarget = 256.0
    maxTarget = 13120.0
    scaledValue = int((angle / ((maxAngle - minAngle) / (maxTarget - minTarget)\
)) + minTarget)
    commandByte = chr(0x84)
    channelByte = chr(channel)
    lowTargetByte = chr(scaledValue & 0x7F)
    highTargetByte = chr((scaledValue >> 7) & 0x7F)
    command = commandByte + channelByte + lowTargetByte + highTargetByte
    ser.write(command)
    ser.flush()

ser = serial.Serial("/dev/ttyACM0", 9600)

# Home position
for i in range(0, 9):
    setAngle(ser, i ,90)

while 1:
    servo = int(raw_input("Servo number: "))
    angle = int(raw_input("Angle: "))
    setAngle(ser, servo, angle)

ser.close()

-UU-:----F1   robot.py        All L1      (Fundamental)-------------------
File mode specification error: (invalid-read-syntax "} or . in a vector")
```

This code includes the Python `setAngle` function from *Chapter 2, Building the Biped*. The specifics were taken from the `www.pololu.com` website, but it simply allows you to set a specific servo to a specific angle.

The next part of the code sets all of the servos to their center location. The final piece of the code, the `while 1:` code set, simply asks the user for a servo and an angle, and then sends the command to the servo controller.

Once the program is run, you should see your biped standing straight up. If not, you may need to center your servos by adjusting the position of the horns. This is a useful pose, but there are others that are more stable. As an excellent first example, you can change the pose to be more like a Tyrannosaurus Rex pose, with knees pointing back. Here are the basic servo positions:

Servo	Angle
1	60
2	60
3	60
6	120
7	120
8	120

The robot pose should look like this:

You can use these angles to achieve this pose. However, this will leave you with some limited movement, as your servos will be toward the end of their ability to move in one direction. As this is going to be the starting pose for your robot, to achieve maximum flexibility, you'll want to center the servos at this position. To do this, run the default, `robot.py`, to set the legs to the center position. Now, adjust the servo horns to achieve this pose while the values of the servos are at a 90 degree angle.

It should look like this:

Now that you have a stable base to work from, you can start programming a simple walking motion.

A basic walking motion

Your robot is poised to walk, however, you first have to get a leg off the ground. Of course, that is easy enough; if you simply lift the leg by changing the angle of the knee joint, your leg can get off the ground. You may also want to change the angle of the front to back ankle; this will allow you to lift the leg without raising it quite as high.

However, you'll have a problem if you change just these two servos; as you lift the leg, your robot will fall over. This is due to a simple principle called the center of gravity. When your robot is at rest, your center of gravity looks like this:

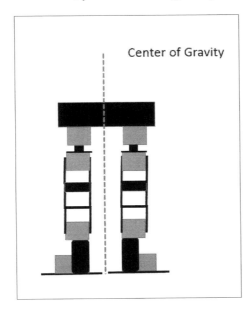

It is clear that if you lift a leg, the robot will fall over in the direction of the leg that has been lifted. What you need to do is to shift the center of gravity over the leg that will be left on the ground using the ankle servo that can tilt the robot left and right, so that it ends up like this:

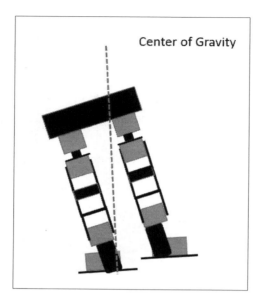

You'll then want to set your servos to lift the left leg. Here is a side view of these servo settings:

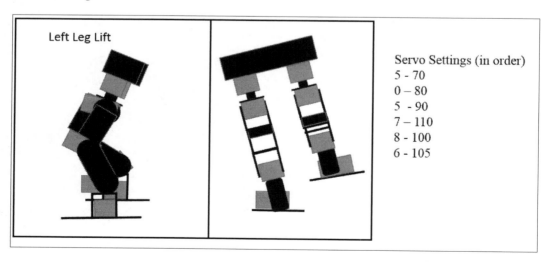

Left Leg Lift

Servo Settings (in order)
5 - 70
0 – 80
5 - 90
7 – 110
8 - 100
6 - 105

Now, it's time for some Python code to make this happen. You'll start with your `robot.py` code and will add the following lines to a function called `liftLeftLeg`:

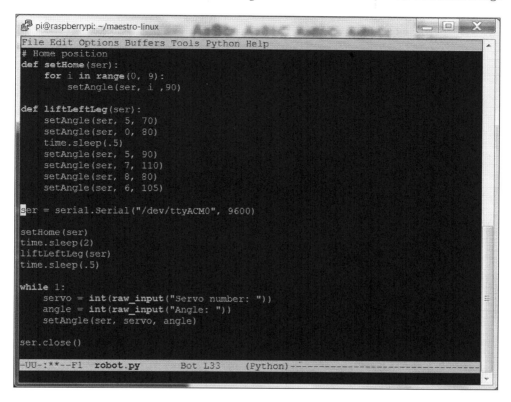

```
pi@raspberrypi: ~/maestro-linux
File Edit Options Buffers Tools Python Help
# Home position
def setHome(ser):
    for i in range(0, 9):
        setAngle(ser, i ,90)

def liftLeftLeg(ser):
    setAngle(ser, 5, 70)
    setAngle(ser, 0, 80)
    time.sleep(.5)
    setAngle(ser, 5, 90)
    setAngle(ser, 7, 110)
    setAngle(ser, 8, 80)
    setAngle(ser, 6, 105)

ser = serial.Serial("/dev/ttyACM0", 9600)

setHome(ser)
time.sleep(2)
liftLeftLeg(ser)
time.sleep(.5)

while 1:
    servo = int(raw_input("Servo number: "))
    angle = int(raw_input("Angle: "))
    setAngle(ser, servo, angle)

ser.close()
-UU-:**--F1   robot.py        Bot L33     (Python)-------------------
```

This will tip the robot onto its right leg, and then lift the left leg, like this:

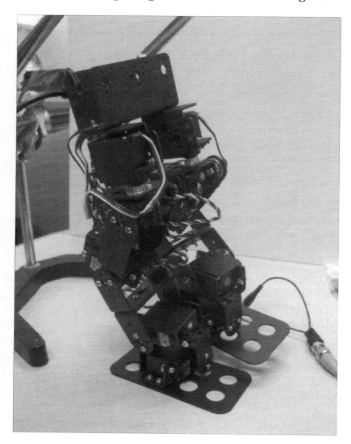

Now, it is fairly easy to step forward. Just move the hip joint on the left leg forward, and then move the ankle joint on the right leg to tip the entire robot forward. Here is the diagram and servo settings:

Step Left Leg Forward

Servo Settings (in order)
8 - 80
7 – 110
6 - 95
3 – 110
2 - 80
1 – 105
0 - 90

Here is the Python code:

```
def liftLeftLeg(ser):
    setAngle(ser, 5, 70)
    setAngle(ser, 0, 80)
    time.sleep(.5)
    setAngle(ser, 5, 90)
    setAngle(ser, 7, 110)
    setAngle(ser, 8, 80)
    setAngle(ser, 6, 105)


def stepLeftForward(ser):
    setAngle(ser, 8, 80)
    setAngle(ser, 7, 100)
    setAngle(ser, 6, 95)
    time.sleep(.5)
    setAngle(ser, 3, 110)
    time.sleep(.5)
    setAngle(ser, 2, 80)
    time.sleep(.5)
    setAngle(ser, 1, 105)
    setAngle(ser, 0, 90)
    time.sleep(.5)
```

pi@raspberrypi: ~/maestro-linux

File Edit Options Buffers Tools Python Help

-UU-:**--F1   robotRex.py   35% L35   (Python)-----------------

Here is a picture of the robot:

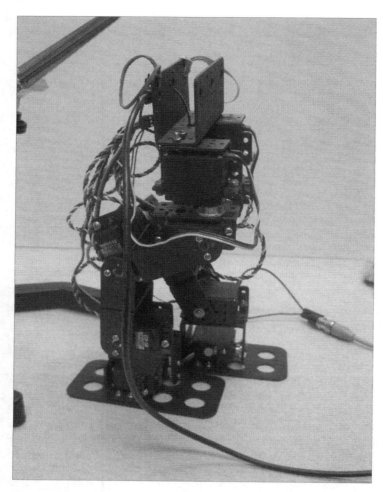

This is the first stage of a walking gait. So, let's detail all the motions you'll need in order to walk your robot forward. Here are the side view diagrams of the different states:

These are the pictures of the robot in each of the different states:

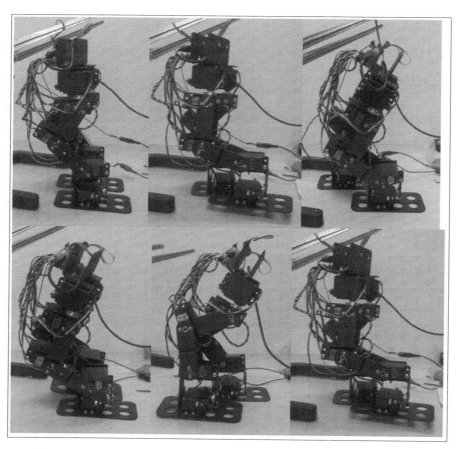

Here is the Python code for each of the functions for the different states:

```
pi@raspberrypi: ~/maestro-linux
File Edit Options Buffers Tools Python Help

def liftLeftLeg(ser):
    setAngle(ser, 5, 70)
    setAngle(ser, 0, 80)
    time.sleep(.5)
    setAngle(ser, 5, 90)
    setAngle(ser, 7, 110)
    setAngle(ser, 8, 80)
    setAngle(ser, 6, 105)
def liftRightLeg(ser):
    setAngle(ser, 0, 110)
    setAngle(ser, 5, 100)
    time.sleep(.1)
    setAngle(ser, 0, 90)
    setAngle(ser, 2, 70)
    setAngle(ser, 3, 100)
    setAngle(ser, 1, 95)
def stepLeftForward(ser):
    setAngle(ser, 8, 80)
    setAngle(ser, 7, 100)
    setAngle(ser, 6, 95)
    time.sleep(.5)
    setAngle(ser, 3, 110)
    time.sleep(.5)
    setAngle(ser, 2, 80)
    time.sleep(.5)
    setAngle(ser, 1, 105)
    setAngle(ser, 0, 90)
    time.sleep(.5)
def stepRightForward(ser):
    setAngle(ser, 3, 80)
    setAngle(ser, 2, 70)
    setAngle(ser, 1, 70)
    time.sleep(.5)
    setAngle(ser, 8, 80)
    time.sleep(.5)
    setAngle(ser, 7, 90)
    time.sleep(.5)
    setAngle(ser, 6, 75)
    time.sleep(.5)
    setAngle(ser, 5, 90)

ser = serial.Serial("/dev/ttyACM0", 9600)

-UU-:----F1   robotRex.py     32% L46    (Python)--------------
```

You'll notice that each function has a number of different servo control statements; these must be performed in this order to get the desired result.

Here is the Python code to sequence the functions for two steps: one with the left leg, and the other with the right leg:

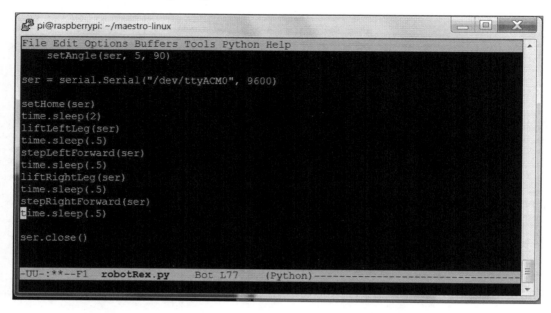

```
    setAngle(ser, 5, 90)

ser = serial.Serial("/dev/ttyACM0", 9600)

setHome(ser)
time.sleep(2)
liftLeftLeg(ser)
time.sleep(.5)
stepLeftForward(ser)
time.sleep(.5)
liftRightLeg(ser)
time.sleep(.5)
stepRightForward(ser)
time.sleep(.5)

ser.close()
```

This is a very simple gait; it's not particularly elegant. You can see that each state is made up of many individual servo moves. You can certainly add more servo moves to make it smoother and more refined. Your exact servo angle settings will certainly vary from these; you'll need to do some experimentation to get your biped's legs positioned correctly.

Now that you can walk, you will also need to teach your robot how to turn.

A basic turn for the robot

Your robot can walk forward, but you'll also want your robot to be able to turn. Your turning is limited to the amount you can turn the hip of your robot, which is around 20 degrees for this robot. So, to perform a full 90 degree turn, you'll need to take the turn in several steps. The big difference here is that when you return to the standing state, you do not want to reset your hip rotation servos to 90 degrees. Here are the diagrams, including several that are rear view, for a turn:

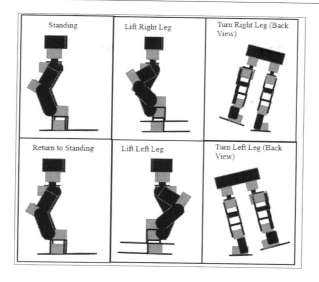

Here is the Python code for a basic turning operation:

```
# Home position
def setHome(ser):
    for i in range(0, 9):
        setAngle(ser, i ,90)
    setAngle(ser, 4, 85)

def setHomeNoHips(ser):
    for i in range(0, 3):
        setAngle(ser, i ,90)
    for i in range(5, 8):
        setAngle(ser, i ,90)

def liftLeftLeg(ser):
    setAngle(ser, 5, 70)
    setAngle(ser, 0, 80)
    time.sleep(.5)
    setAngle(ser, 5, 90)
    setAngle(ser, 7, 110)
    setAngle(ser, 8, 80)
    setAngle(ser, 6, 105)
def liftRightLeg(ser):
    setAngle(ser, 0, 110)
    setAngle(ser, 5, 100)
    time.sleep(.1)
    setAngle(ser, 0, 90)
    setAngle(ser, 2, 70)
    setAngle(ser, 3, 100)
    setAngle(ser, 1, 90)
def turnLeftLegLeftCenter(ser):
    setAngle(ser, 9, 80)
def turnRightLegRightCenter(ser):
    setAngle(ser, 9, 100)

ser = serial.Serial("/dev/ttyACM0", 9600)
```

And here is the Python code to chain these basic states together to step a turn:

```
pi@raspberrypi: ~/maestro-linux
File Edit Options Buffers Tools Python Help
ser = serial.Serial("/dev/ttyACM0", 9600)

setHome(ser)
time.sleep(2)
liftLeftLeg(ser)
time.sleep(.5)
turnLeftLegLeftCenter(ser)
time.sleep(.5)
setHomeNoHips(ser)
time.sleep(.5)
liftRightLeg(ser)
time.sleep(.5)
turnRightLegRightCenter(ser)
time.sleep(.5)
setHome(ser)
time.sleep(.5)

-UU-:----F1   robotRex.py      76% L52     (Python)----------------------
```

Now your robot can walk and turn! Obviously, your robot could walk backward by reversing the order of servo control statements in each of the functions. There are many more types of motions you can program with your robot, following the planning method outlined in this chapter.

Summary

Now, your robot is mobile. The next step is to add some sensors so that your robot can avoid, or find, objects in its path.

4
Avoiding Obstacles Using Sensors

You've constructed your biped robot. Now, your robot can move around. But what if you want the robot to sense the outside world, so you don't run into things? In this chapter, you'll discover how to add some sensors to help avoid barriers.

Specifically, you'll learn:

- How to connect Raspberry Pi to an **IR (infrared)** sensor
- How to connect Raspberry Pi to a USB **sonar sensor** to detect the world
- How to connect Raspberry Pi and its GPIO to a sonar sensor to detect the world

Connecting Raspberry Pi to an infrared sensor

Your robot can now move around, but you'll want to be able to sense a barrier or a target. One of the ways to do this is with an IR sensor. First, a tutorial on IR sensors is required. An IR sensor has both a transmitter and a sensor. The transmitter sends out a narrow beam of light, and the sensor receives this beam of light.

The difference in transit ends up as an angle measurement in the sensor, as shown in the following figure:

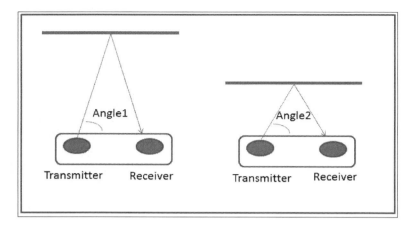

The different angles give you an indication of the distance from the object. The sensor turns these angle measurements into a voltage that you can sense to determine the distance. Unfortunately, the relationship between the output of the sensor and the distance is not linear, so you'll need to do some calibration in order to predict the actual distance and its relationship to the output of the sensor.

IR sensors are quite accurate, certainly with a low percentage of errors; however, they may not work well if the area is brightly lit. The accuracy is also affected by the reflective nature of the material being sensed. This can be a consideration when deciding which sensors to use.

Before you get started, you'll need to get a sensor. One of the more popular ones is an inexpensive IR sensor by Sharp. It is available at many online electronics stores, and it comes in models that sense various distances. You'll be using the **Sharp 2Y0A02** model, a unit that provides sensing to a distance of 150 cm. Here is a picture of the sensor:

You'll also want to make sure you also get the connector cable for the device; it normally comes with the device. Here is a picture of the sensor with the cable attached:

As noted in the tutorial, the voltage out of the sensor will be a voltage that will be an indication of the distance. However, this is an analog signal, and the Raspberry Pi doesn't have an analog-to-digital converter that can convert this analog voltage to a number that you can read in your program. You'll need to add an analog to digital converter to your project.

There are two choices. If you want an analog-to-digital converter that plugs directly into the USB interface, there is one offered by www.phidgets.com. This board is really quite amazing; it takes the analog signals, turns them into digital numbers using an analog to digital converter, and then makes them available so that they can be read from the USB port. The model number of this part is **1011_0 - PhidgetInterfaceKit 2/2/2** and it is shown in the following:

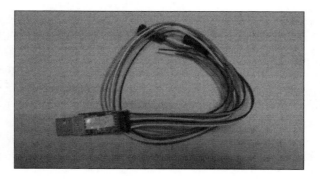

Unfortunately, it takes a bit of programming expertise to get it up and running. The other choice is to use an analog-to-digital converter that connects to the GPIO pins of the Raspberry Pi. There is a part, the **ADC pi+** from www.abelectronics.co.uk, that does this. It is pictured here:

This device is easier to program, so this is what you'll use in this project. Now, let's connect the sensor:

1. Solder header pins to the ADC Pi+ board to connect it to the ADC, like this:

2. Now, plug the board into the Raspberry Pi B 2. Here is a picture of the combination:

3. Now, you'll connect the IR sensor to the ADC. To connect this unit, you'll connect the three pins that are available at the bottom of the sensor. Here is the connection list:

ADC-DAC Board	Sensor Pin
5V	Vcc
GND	Gnd
In1	Vo

Unfortunately, there are no labels on the unit, but here are the pins you'll connect:

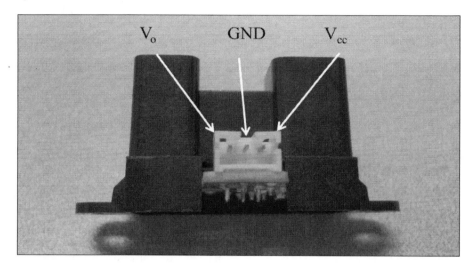

It's easiest to connect to the three-wire cable that normally comes with the sensor. Once the pins are connected, you are ready to access the data from the sensor via a Python program on the Raspberry Pi. The entire system looks like this:

Now, you are ready to add some code to read the IR sensor. You'll need to follow these steps to talk to the ADC:

1. The first step in enabling the ADC is to enable the I2C interface. This is done by running `raspi-config` and selecting **8 Advanced Options** like this:

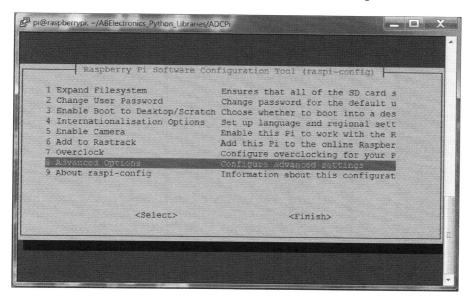

2. Once there, go to the **A7 I2C** selection to enable the I2C like this:

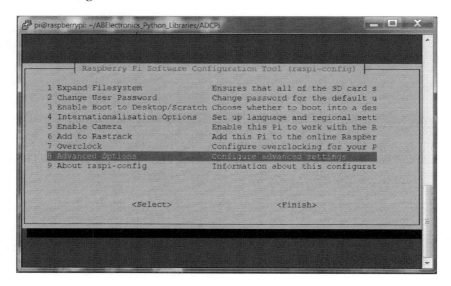

Perform all the selections to enable the I2C interface and load the library, and then reboot the Raspberry Pi.

You'll also need to edit the /etc/modules file and add the following two lines:

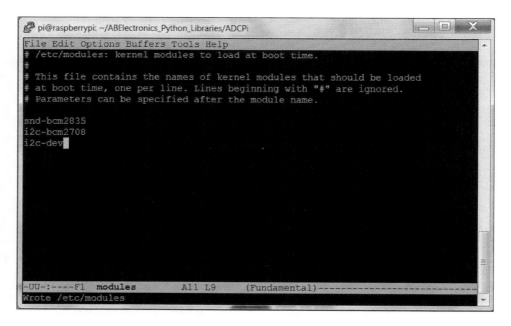

Reboot the Raspberry Pi. You can see whether the I2C is enabled by typing `sudo i2cdetect -y 1`, and you should see something like this:

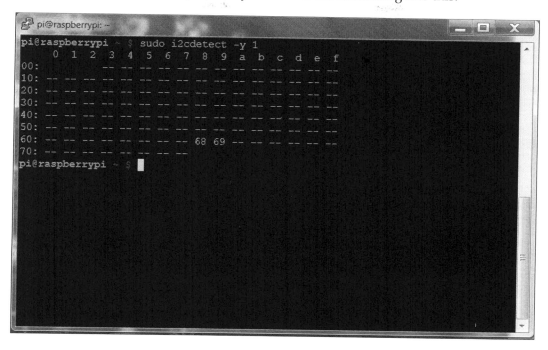

The I2C device, your ADC, is available at the **68** and **69** addresses.

3. Now, you can download the code. To do this, type `git clone https://github.com/abelectronicsuk/ABElectronics_Python_Libraries.git` from the home directory, and the Python libraries will be installed on your Raspberry Pi.

4. Go to the `./ABElecttronics_Python_Libraries/ADCPi` directory; here are the programs for your specific hardware. Following the instructions in the `README.md` file, type `sudo apt-get update`, and then type `sudo apt-get install python-smbus`. This will install the `smbus` library, which are required for the ADC to work. Also, type `sudo adduser pi i2c` to add `pi` to the group that can access i2c.

5. You'll need to edit your `.bashrc` file in your home directory, adding the following lines:

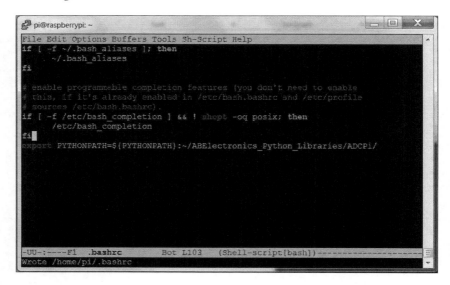

Adding this line will add this library to the path so that you can access the functionality. Reboot the Raspberry Pi.

6. Now, you can run one of the demo programs. Type python demo-readvoltage.py, and you should see something like this:

![terminal output](data:)

```
Channel 1: 0.225269
Channel 2: 0.000000
Channel 3: 0.000000
Channel 4: 0.000000
Channel 5: 0.000000
Channel 6: 0.000000
Channel 7: 0.000000
Channel 8: 0.000000
```

These raw readings are great, but now you'll want to build a program that takes the data from the first ADC and translates it to the distance. To do this, you'll need a graph of the voltage to distance readings for your sensor. Here is the graph for the IR sensor in this example:

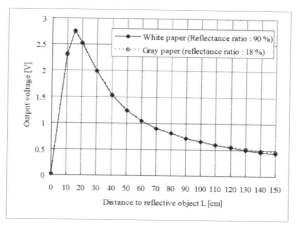

There are really two parts to the curve; the first is the distance up to about 15 centimeters, and the second is the distance from 15 centimeters to 150 centimeters. It is easiest to build a simple mathematical model that ignores distances closer than 15 centimeters and models the distance from 15 centimeters. For more information on how to build this model, refer to http://davstott.me.uk/index.php/2013/06/02/raspberry-pi-sharp-infrared/. Here is the Python program using this model:

```
#!/usr/bin/python

from ABE_ADCPi import ADCPi
from ABE_helpers import ABEHelpers
import time
import os

i2c_helper = ABEHelpers()
bus = i2c_helper.get_smbus()
adc = ADCPi(bus, 0x68, 0x69, 12)

while (True):
    distance = (1.0 / (adc.read_voltage(1)/13.15)) - 0.35
    print ("Distance", distance)
    time.sleep(0.5)
```

The only new line of code is the distance = (1.0 / (adc.read_adc_voltage(1) / 13.15)) - 0.35 line. It converts your voltage to distance. You can now run your program and you'll see the results in centimeters, like this:

```
pi@raspberrypi: ~
('Distance', 11.004038054968285)
('Distance', 10.932478991596637)
('Distance', 11.125341880341878)
('Distance', 10.932478991596637)
('Distance', 8.134139020537123)
('Distance', 6.878075370121129)
('Distance', 7.161132867132867)
('Distance', 7.1927808988764035)
('Distance', 7.1927808988764035)
('Distance', 5.7736716077537045)
('Distance', 5.226801661474558)
('Distance', 5.226801661474558)
('Distance', 4.99906374501992)
('Distance', 5.004396809571285)
('Distance', 5.102243654822335)
('Distance', 8.215326953748004)
('Distance', 10.932478991596637)
('Distance', 11.324913043478258)
('Distance', 12.653535108958835)
('Distance', 13.420410256410255)
('Distance', 59.321777777777775)
('Distance', 59.321777777777775)
('Distance', 59.992247191011224)
```

Now, you can measure the distance to objects using your IR sensor!

Connecting Raspberry Pi to a USB sonar sensor

There is yet another way to sense the presence of objects: using a sonar sensor. But before you add this capability to your system, here's a little tutorial on sonar sensors. This type of sensor uses ultrasonic sound to calculate the distance from an object. The sound wave travels out from the sensor, as illustrated in the following figure:

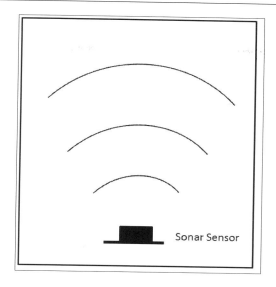

The device sends out a sound wave 10 times a second. If an object is in the path of these waves, then the waves reflect off the object, sending waves that return to the sensor, as shown in the following figure:

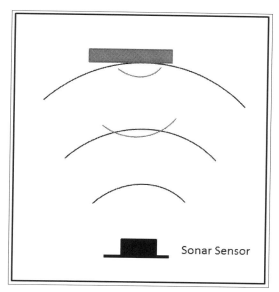

The sensor then measures any return. It uses the time difference between when the sound wave was sent out and when it returned to measure the distance from the object.

Sonar sensors are also quite accurate, normally with low percentage errors, and are not affected by the lighting or color in the environment.

There are several choices if you want to use a sonar sensor to sense the distance. The first is to use a sonar sensor that connects to the USB port. The following is an image of a USB sonar sensor:

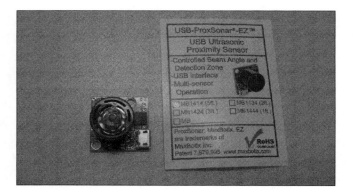

This is the **USB-ProxSonar-EZ** sensor, and can be purchased directly from MaxBotix or on Amazon. There are several models, each with a different distance specification; however, they all work in the same way.

You can also choose a sonar sensor that connects to the GPIO of the Raspberry Pi. Here is a picture of this sort of inexpensive sonar sensor:

This sensor is less expensive and easy to use; it takes a bit of processing power to coordinate the efforts of timing the send and receive signals, but the Raspberry Pi B 2 has the processing power needed. Here are the steps to set up this sonar sensor to sense the distance:

1. The first step is to understand the GPIO pins of the Raspberry Pi B 2. Here is a diagram of the layout of the pins:

Pin 1 3.3V	□ ○	Pin 2 5V
Pin 3 GPIO2	○ ○	Pin 4 5V
Pin 5 GPIO3	○ ○	Pin 6 GND
Pin 7 GPIO4	○ ○	Pin 8 GPIO14
Pin 9 GND	○ ○	Pin 10 GPIO15
Pin 11 GPIO17	○ ○	Pin 12 GPIO18
Pin 13 GPIO27	○ ○	Pin 14 GND
Pin 15 GPIO22	○ ○	Pin 16 GPIO23
Pin 17 3.3V	○ ○	Pin 18 GPIO24
Pin 19 GPIO10	○ ○	Pin 20 GND
Pin 21 GPIO9	○ ○	Pin 22 GPIO25
Pin 23 GPIO11	○ ○	Pin 24 GPIO8
Pin 25 GND	○ ○	Pin 26 GPIO7
Pin 27 ID_SD	○ ○	Pin 28 ID_SC
Pin 29 GPIO5	○ ○	Pin 30 GND
Pin 31 GPIO6	○ ○	Pin 32 GPIO12
Pin 33 GPIO13	○ ○	Pin 34 GND
Pin 35 GPIO19	○ ○	Pin 36 GPIO16
Pin 37 GPIO26	○ ○	Pin 38 GPIO20
Pin 39 GND	○ ○	Pin 40 GPIO21

In this case, you'll need to connect to the 5 volt connection of the Raspberry Pi B2, which is pin 2. You'll also need to connect to the GND, which is pin 6. You'll use pin 16 as an output trigger pin and pin 18 (GPIO24) as an input to time the echo from the sonar sensor.

2. Now that you know the pins you'll connect to, you can connect the sonar sensor. There is a problem, as you can't connect the 5 volt return from the sonar sensor directly to the Raspberry Pi GPIO pins; they want 3.3 volts. You'll need to build a voltage divider that will reduce the 5 volts to 3.3 volts. This can be done with two resistors, which are connected as shown in this diagram:

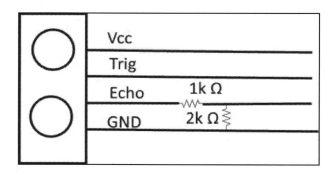

If you'd like more information on how the voltage divider works in this configuration, refer to `http://www.modmypi.com/blog/hc-sr04-ultrasonic-range-sensor-on-the-raspberry-pi`. The combination of these two resistors will reduce the voltage to the desired levels. You may want to put all of this is in a small breadboard, as shown here:

Finally, connect it to the Raspberry Pi, like this:

3. Now that the device is connected, you'll need a bit of code to read in the value, make sure it is settled (a stable measurement), and then convert it to distance. Here is the Python code for this program:

```
import RPi.GPIO as GPIO
import time
GPIO.setmode(GPIO.BCM)

trig_pin = 23
echo_pin = 24
GPIO.setup(trig_pin,GPIO.OUT)
GPIO.setup(echo_pin,GPIO.IN)

GPIO.output(trig_pin, False)
print "Waiting to settle"
time.sleep(1)
GPIO.output(trig_pin, True)
time.sleep(0.00001)
GPIO.output(trig_pin, False)

while GPIO.input(echo_pin)==0:
    start = time.time()

while GPIO.input(echo_pin)==1:
    end = time.time()

duration = end - start
distance = duration * 17150
distance = round(distance, 2)
print "Distance:",distance,"cm"
GPIO.cleanup()
```

Now, you should be able to run the program and see a result, like this:

Now that you have your sensors up and working, you can avoid or find objects with your biped.

Summary

Congratulations! You can now detect and avoid walls and other barriers to your robot. You can also use these sensors to detect objects that you might want to find. In the next chapter, you'll learn how to perform path planning to move your robot from point A to point B and even give your robot intelligence as to what to do if it encounters a barrier in its path.

5
Path Planning and Your Biped

Now that your biped is up and mobile and able to find barriers, you can now start to have it move around autonomously. However, you'll want to have your robot planed his path, that is, if it knows where it has started and the desired end point, it can move from the starting point to the end point.

In this chapter, you will be learning about:

- How to add a compass to your biped, so you'll have a sense of direction
- Learning some basic path planning techniques for your robot

Connecting a digital compass to the Raspberry Pi

One of the important pieces of information that might be useful for your robot, it if is going to plan its own path, is its direction of travel. So, let's learn how to hook up a digital compass to the Raspberry Pi.

There are several chips that provide digital compass capability; one of the most common is the **HMC5883L 3-Axis Digital Compass chip**. This chip is packaged onto a module by several companies, but almost all of them result in a similar interface. The following is a picture of one the **GY-271 HMC5883L Triple Axis Compass Magnetometer Sensor Module**, which is available from a number of online retailers:

This type of digital compass uses magnetic sensors to discover the earth's magnetic field. The output of these sensors is then made accessible to the outside world through a set of registers that allow the user to set things such as the sample rate, and continuous or single sampling. The x, y, and z directions are output-using registers as well.

The connections to this chip are straightforward and the device communicates with the Raspberry Pi by using the I2C bus, a standard serial communications bus. The I2C interface is a synchronous serial interface and provides more performance than an asynchronous Rx/Tx serial interface. The SCL data line provides a clock, while the data flows on the SDA line. The bus also provides addressing so that more than one device can be connected to the master device at the same time. On the back of the module, the connections are labeled, as shown in the following image:

You'll then connect the device to the GPIO pins on Raspberry Pi. The following is the pin out of Raspberry Pi:

Pin 1 3.3V			Pin 2 5V
Pin 3 GPIO2			Pin 4 5V
Pin 5 GPIO3			Pin 6 GND
Pin 7 GPIO4			Pin 8 GPIO14
Pin 9 GND			Pin 10 GPIO15
Pin 11 GPIO17			Pin 12 GPIO18
Pin 13 GPIO27			Pin 14 GND
Pin 15 GPIO22			Pin 16 GPIO23
Pin 17 3.3V			Pin 18 GPIO24
Pin 19 GPIO10			Pin 20 GND
Pin 21 GPIO9			Pin 22 GPIO25
Pin 23 GPIO11			Pin 24 GPIO8
Pin 25 GND			Pin 26 GPIO7
Pin 27 ID_SD			Pin 28 ID_SC
Pin 29 GPIO5			Pin 30 GND
Pin 31 GPIO6			Pin 32 GPIO12
Pin 33 GPIO13			Pin 34 GND
Pin 35 GPIO19			Pin 36 GPIO16
Pin 37 GPIO26			Pin 38 GPIO20
Pin 39 GND			Pin 40 GPIO21

Connect your device to the VCC on the device to Pin 1 (3.3 V) on Raspberry Pi. Connect GND to Pin 9 (GND). Connect SCL on the device to Pin 5 (GPIO 3) and SDA to Pin 3 (GPIO 2) on the device. Notice that you will not connect the **Data Ready (DRDY)** line. Now, you are ready to communicate with the device.

Accessing the compass programmatically

In order to access the compass capability, you'll need to enable the I2C library on Raspberry. If you used the IR sensor and ADC additional hardware in *Chapter 4, Avoiding Obstacles Using Sensors*, you will have already done this. If not, follow these instructions to enable the I2C interface:

1. Run `raspi-config`. Select the **Configure advanced settings**, as shown in the following screenshot:

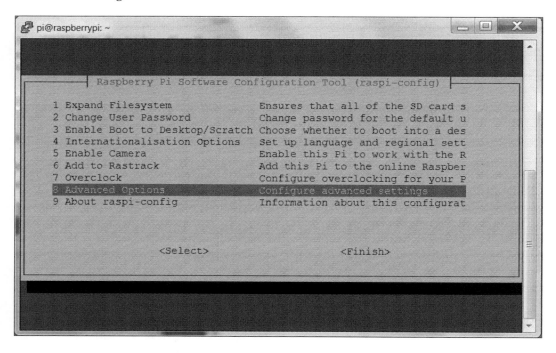

From the next selection page, select the Enable/disable automatic loading of the I2C interface, as shown in the following screenshot:

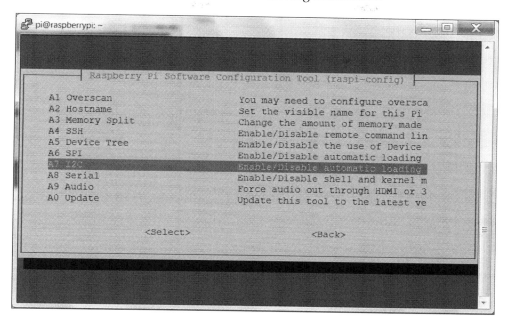

Then select **yes**, as shown in the following screenshot:

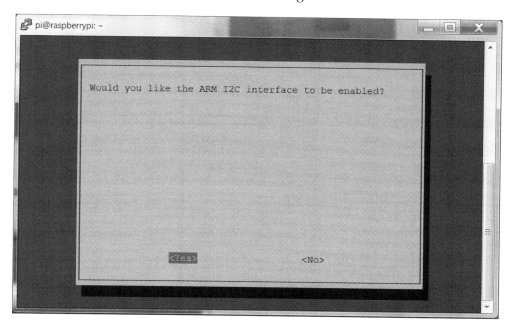

You'll also want to edit the file `/etc/modules` and add the lines `i2c-bcm2708` and `i2c-dev`, as shown in the following screenshot:

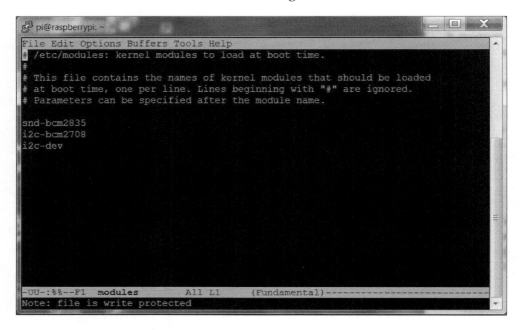

And one final edit, change the last line in `/boot/config.txt`, as shown in the following screenshot:

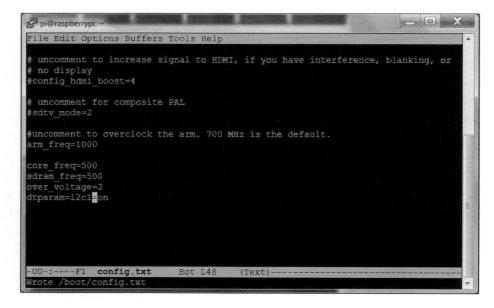

Now, reboot Raspberry Pi.

2. With the device connected, you can see if the system knows about your device. To do this, type the following command:

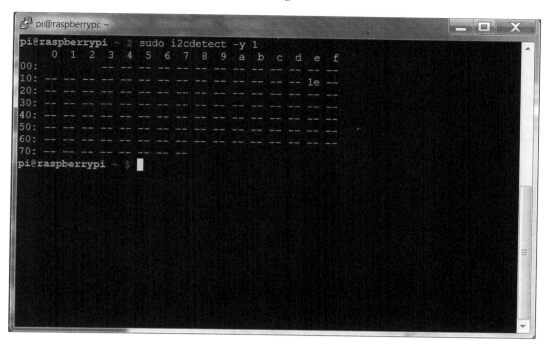

You can see the device at **1e**.

3. Now you communicate with your digital compass. To do this, you'll need to create a Python program. But before you create your Python code, you'll want to download a library that will make this all much easier. To do this, first create a directory a directory called `compass` and `cd` to that directory. Then, type `git clone https://github.com/quick2wire/quick2wire-python-api.git` to download the `quick2wire-python-api` library. Finally, type `git clone https://bitbucket.org/thinkbowl/i2clibraries.git` to get the i2clibraries.

You'll also need to set some environment variables. Do this by going to your home directory and editing the `.bashrc` file, adding these two lines at the end:

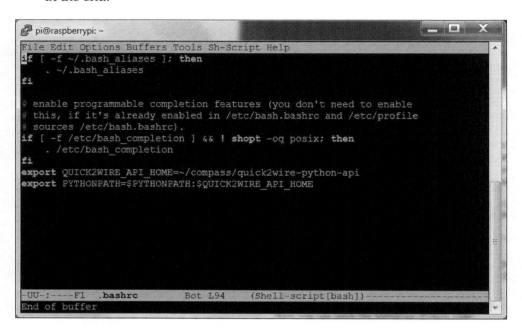

4. Now, you can create the following Python code:

5. Now, run the code by typing `python3 compass.py` command and you should see:

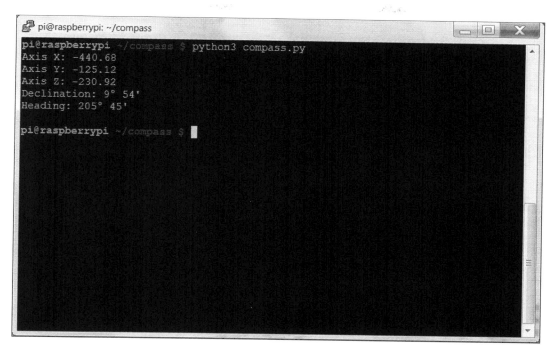

```
pi@raspberrypi: ~/compass
pi@raspberrypi ~/compass $ python3 compass.py
Axis X: -440.68
Axis Y: -125.12
Axis Z: -230.92
Declination: 9° 54'
Heading: 205° 45'

pi@raspberrypi ~/compass $
```

Now, you can add direction to your project! As you move the device around, you should see the **Heading** value change.

> This is a basic program; you can find out more about other features that are available with this library at http://think-bowl.com/ raspberry-pi/i2c-python-library-3-axis-digital- compass-hmc5883l-with-the-raspberry-pi/.

One final step in developing your compass code is to make it a file where the functions can then be imported to a different Python program. To do this, edit the file so that all of the code is in functions, as shown by the following:

```python
#!/usr/bin/python
import smbus
import time
import math

bus = smbus.SMBus(1)
address = 0x1e

def read_byte(adr):
    return bus.read_byte_data(address, adr)

def read_word(adr):
    high = bus.read_byte_data(address, adr)
    low = bus.read_byte_data(address, adr+1)
    val = (high << 8) + low
    return val

def read_word_2c(adr):
    val = read_word(adr)
    if (val >= 0x8000):
        return -((65535 - val) + 1)
    else:
        return val

def write_byte(adr, value):
    bus.write_byte_data(address, adr, value)

def getReading():
    write_byte(0, 0b01110000) # Set to 8 samples @ 15Hz
    write_byte(1, 0b00100000) # 1.3 gain LSb / Gauss 1090 (default)
    write_byte(2, 0b00000000) # Continuous sampling
    scale = 0.92
    x_out = read_word_2c(3) * scale
    y_out = read_word_2c(7) * scale
    z_out = read_word_2c(5) * scale
    bearing  = math.atan2(y_out, x_out)
    if (bearing < 0):
        bearing += 2 * math.pi
    bearing = math.degrees(bearing)
    return bearing
```

-UU-:----F1   **compass.py**   All L1   (Python)------------------
For information about GNU Emacs and the GNU system, type C-h C-a.

Then you'll be able to use the import capability of Python to import this functionality into a different Python file.

Dynamic path planning for your robot

Now that you can see barriers and also know direction, you'll want to do dynamic path planning. Dynamic path planning simply means that you don't have a knowledge of the entire world with all the possible barriers before you encounter them. Your robot will have to decide how to proceed while it is in the middle and actually moving. This can be a complex topic, but there are some basics that you can start to understand and apply as you ask your robot to move around its environment. Let's first address the problem of knowing where you want to go and needing to execute a path without barriers, and then adding in barriers.

Basic path planning

In order to talk about dynamic path planning, that is, planning a path where you don't know what barriers you might encounter, you'll need a framework to understand where your robot is as well as to determine the location of the goal. One common framework is an *x-y* grid. The following is a drawing of such a grid:

There are three key points:

- The lower left point is a fixed reference position. The directions x and y are also fixed, and all other positions will be measured with respect to this position and these directions.

- Another important point is the starting location of your robot. Your robot will then keep track of its location by using its x coordinate, or position itself with respect to some fixed reference position in the x direction, and its y coordinate, its position with respect to some fixed reference position in the y direction to the goal. It will use the compass to keep track of these directions.

- The third important point is the position of the goal, also given in x and y coordinates with respect to the fixed reference position. If you know the starting location and the starting angle of your robot ,you can plan an optimum (shortest distance) path to this goal. To do this, you can use the goal location and the robot location, and some fairly simple math to calculate the distance and angle from the robot to the goal.

To calculate the distance, use the following equation:

$$d = \sqrt{\left(\left(X\,goal - X\,goal \right)^2 + \left(Y\,goal - Y\,robot \right)^2 \right)}$$

Use the following equation to tell your robot how far to travel to the goal. A second equation will tell your robot the angle it needs to travel:

$$\theta = \arctan\left(\frac{Y\,goal - Y\,robot}{X\,goal - X\,goal} \right)$$

The following is a graphical representation of these two pieces of information:

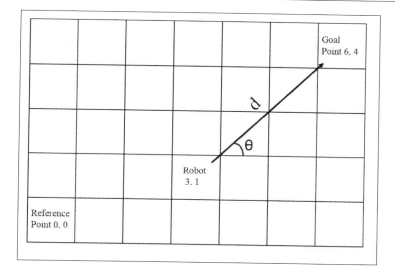

Now that you have a goal angle and distance, you can program your robot to move. To do this, you will write a program to do path planning and call the movement functions that you created in *Chapter 3, Motion for the Biped*. You will, however, need to know the distance that your robot travels in a step so that you can tell your robot how far to travel in steps, not distance units.

You'll also need to be able to translate the distance that might be covered by your robot in a turn; however, this distance may be too small to be of any importance. If you then know the angle and the distance, you can move your robot to the goal.

The following are the steps you will program:

1. Calculate the distance in units that your robot will need to travel in order to reach the goal. Convert this to number of steps to achieve this distance.

2. Calculate the angle that your robot will need to travel to reach the goal. You'll use the compass and your robot turn functions in order to achieve this angle.

3. Now, call the step functions the proper number of times required to move your robot the correct distance.

That's it. Now, we will use some very simple Python code that executes this by using functions to move the robot forward and turn the robot. In this case, it makes sense to create a file called robotLib.py with all of the functions that do the actual servo settings to step the biped robot forward and turn the robot. You'll then import these functions using the from robotLib import * statement, and your Python program can call these functions. This makes the path planning Python program much smaller and more manageable. You'll do the same thing with the compass program, using the from compass import * command.

For more information on how to import the functions from one Python file to another, refer to http://www.tutorialspoint.com/python/python_modules.htm.

The following is a listing of the program:

```
#!/usr/bin/python
import serial
import time
from robotLib import *
from compass import *
import math

ser = serial.Serial("/dev/ttyACM0", 9600)

setHome(ser)
time.sleep(2)

xpos_robot = int(raw_input("Robot X Position: "))
ypos_robot = int(raw_input("Robot Y Position: "))
xpos_goal = int(raw_input("Goal X Position: "))
ypos_goal = int(raw_input("Goal Y Position: "))

distance = math.sqrt((xpos_goal - ypos_robot)**2 + (ypos_goal - ypos_robot)**2)
angle = round(math.degrees(math.atan2((ypos_goal - ypos_robot), (xpos_goal - xp\
os_robot))))
if angle < 0:
    angle = angle + 360
print distance, angle
bearing = getReading()
print bearing, angle
# Turn to the right bearing
while math.fabs(bearing - angle) > 2:
    if (angle) < 180:
        turnRight(ser)
    else:
        turnLeft(ser)
    bearing = getReading()
    print bearing, angle
#Walk the right number of steps - Assume distance = number of steps
while distance > 1:
    stepRightLeg(ser)
    stepLeftLeg(ser)
    distance = distance - 1
    print distance
ser.close()
```

-UU-:----F1 robotGoal.py All L1 (Python)------------------

In this program, the user enters the goal location and the robot first decides the shortest direction to the desired angle by reading the angle. To make it simple, the robot is placed in the grid with it heading in the direction of angle 0. If the goal angle is less than 180 degrees, the robot will turn right. If it is greater than 180 degrees, the robot will turn left. The robot turns until the desired angle and its measured angle are within a few degrees. Then, the robot takes the number of steps to reach the goal.

Avoiding obstacles

Planning paths without obstacles, as has been shown, is quite easy. However, it becomes a bit more challenging when your robot needs to walk around obstacles. Let's look at an instance where there is an obstacle in the path that you calculated previously. It might look like the following:

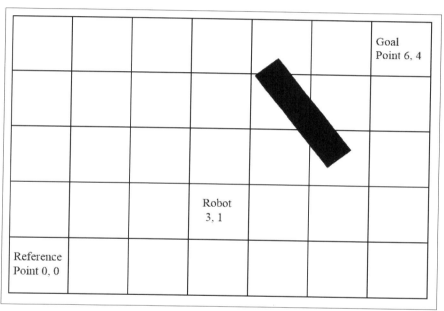

You can still use the same path planning algorithm to find the starting angle; however, you'll now need to use your sonar sensor to detect the obstacle. When your sonar sensor detects the obstacle, you'll need to stop and recalculate a path to avoid the barrier, and then recalculate the desired path to the goal. One very simple way to do this, when your robot senses a barrier, is to turn right 90 degrees, go a fixed distance, and then recalculate the optimum path. When you turn back to move toward the target, if you sense no barrier, you will be able to move along the optimum path.

However, if your robot encounters the obstacle again, it will repeat the process, until it reaches the goal. In this case, using these rules, the robot will travel the following path:

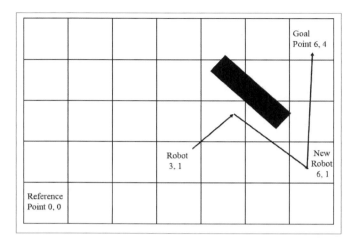

There is one more step you'll need to take before adding the sonar sensor's capability to your robot. You'll need to change the sonar sensor code so that it can be added to the Python code as a library. The following is that code:

```python
import RPi.GPIO as GPIO
import time
GPIO.setmode(GPIO.BCM)

def getDistance():
    trig_pin = 23
    echo_pin = 24
    GPIO.setup(trig_pin,GPIO.OUT)
    GPIO.setup(echo_pin,GPIO.IN)

    GPIO.output(trig_pin, False)
    time.sleep(1)
    GPIO.output(trig_pin, True)
    time.sleep(0.00001)
    GPIO.output(trig_pin, False)

    while GPIO.input(echo_pin)==0:
        start = time.time()

    while GPIO.input(echo_pin)==1:
        end = time.time()

    duration = end - start
    distance = duration * 17150
    distance = round(distance, 2)
    GPIO.cleanup()
    return distance

print "Distance: ", getDistance(), "cm"
```

You'll also import this code using the `from compass import *` statement. You'll also be using the time library and the `time.sleep` command to add delay between different statements in the code. And the following is the first part of the code that uses all of this to detect the barrier, turn to the right, then first part of the Python code that utilizes the sonar sensor:

```
pi@raspberrypi: ~/maestro-linux
File Edit Options Buffers Tools Python Help
#!/usr/bin/python
import serial
import time
from robotLib import *
from compass import *
import math

ser = serial.Serial("/dev/ttyACM0", 9600)

setHome(ser)
time.sleep(2)

xpos_robot = int(raw_input("Robot X Position: "))
ypos_robot = int(raw_input("Robot Y Position: "))
xpos_goal = int(raw_input("Goal X Position: "))
ypos_goal = int(raw_input("Goal Y Position: "))

distance = math.sqrt((xpos_goal - ypos_robot)**2 + (ypos_goal - ypos_robot)**2)
angle = round(math.degrees(math.atan2((ypos_goal - ypos_robot), (xpos_goal - xpos_robot))))
if angle < 0:
    angle = angle + 360
print distance, angle
bearing = getReading()
print bearing, angle

# Turn to the right bearing
while math.fabs(bearing - angle) > 2:
    if (angle) < 180:
        turnRight(ser)
    else:
        turnLeft(ser)
    bearing = getReading()
    print bearing, angle

# Walk the right number of steps - Assume distance = number of steps
-UU-:**--F1  robotBarrier.py   Top L35    (Python)---------------------
Beginning of buffer
```

And the following is the final piece of the code:

```python
#!/usr/bin/python
import serial
import time
from robotLib import *
from compass import *
import math

ser = serial.Serial("/dev/ttyACM0", 9600)

setHome(ser)
time.sleep(2)

xpos_robot = int(raw_input("Robot X Position: "))
ypos_robot = int(raw_input("Robot Y Position: "))
xpos_goal = int(raw_input("Goal X Position: "))
ypos_goal = int(raw_input("Goal Y Position: "))

distance = math.sqrt((xpos_goal - ypos_robot)**2 + (ypos_goal - ypos_robot)**2)
angle = round(math.degrees(math.atan2((ypos_goal - ypos_robot), (xpos_goal - xpos_robot))))
if angle < 0:
    angle = angle + 360
print distance, angle
bearing = getReading()
print bearing, angle

# Turn to the right bearing
while math.fabs(bearing - angle) > 2:
    if (angle) < 180:
        turnRight(ser)
    else:
        turnLeft(ser)
    bearing = getReading()
    print bearing, angle

#Walk the right number of steps - Assume distance = number of steps
```

Now, this algorithm is quite simple; there are others that have much more complex responses to barriers. You can also see that by adding sonar sensors to the sides your robot could actually sense when the barrier has ended. You could also provide more complex decision processes about which way to turn to avoid an object. Again, there are many different path finding algorithms. See `http://www.academia.edu/837604/A_Simple_Local_Path_Planning_Algorithm_for_Autonomous_Mobile_Robots` for an example of this. These more complex algorithms can be explored by using the basic functionality that you have built in this chapter.

Summary

You've now added path planning to your robot's capability. Your robot can now not only move from point A to point B, but can also avoid barriers that might be in the way. In the next chapter, you'll learn how to add a webcam to your biped. This will introduce a whole new set of ways for your robot to experience the world around it.

6
Adding Vision to Your Biped

Now that your biped is up and mobile, is able to find barriers, and knows how to plan its path, you can now start to have it move around autonomously. However, you may want your robot to follow a color or motion.

In this chapter, you will be learning:

- How to add a webcam to your biped robot
- How to add RaspiCam to your biped robot
- How to install and use OpenCV, an open source vision package
- How to follow motion with your biped robot

Installing a camera on your biped robot

Having vision capability is a real advantage for your biped robot; you'll use this functionality in lots of different applications. Fortunately, adding hardware and software for vision is both easy and inexpensive. There are two choices as far as vision hardware is concerned. You can add a USB webcam to your system, or you can add RaspiCam, a camera designed specifically for Raspberry Pi.

Installing a USB camera on Raspberry Pi

Connecting a USB camera is very easy. Just plug it into the USB slot. To make sure that your device is connected, type `lsusb`. You should see the following:

This shows a Creative Webcam located at Bus 001 Device 004: ID 041e:4095. To make sure that the system sees this as a video device, type `ls /dev/v*` command and you should see something like the following:

The /dev/video0 is the webcam device. Now that your device is connected, let's actually see if you can capture images and video. There are several tools that can allow you to access the webcam, but a simple program with video controls is called luvcview. To install this, type `sudo apt-get install luvcview`. Once the application is installed, you'll want to run it. To do this, you'll either need to be connected directly to a display or able to access Raspberry Pi via a remote VNC connection, such as vncserver, as displaying images will require a graphical interface.

Once you are connected in this manner, open a terminal window on Raspberry Pi and run `luvcview`. You should see something like the following:

Don't worry about the quality of the image, you'll be capturing and processing your images inside of OpenCV, a vision framework.

Installing RaspiCam on Raspberry Pi

The other choice for seeing the outside world on Raspberry Pi is to use the RaspiCam. Installing this camera is a bit more involved; you are going to connect it to a special connector on the Raspberry Pi. The following is a picture of the camera with its special connector:

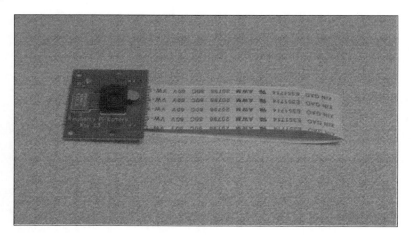

You may also want to add the protective cover for the camera; assembling it looks like the following:

Now you are ready to connect the camera to Raspberry Pi. The camera connects to the Raspberry Pi by installing it into the connector marked Camera on the Raspberry Pi. To see how this is done, see the video at `http://www.raspberrypi.org/help/camera-module-setup/`.

Now that the camera is connected, you'll want to enable the camera using the `raspi-config` utility. Type `sudo raspi-config`, then select the **Enable Camera**, as shown in the following screenshot:

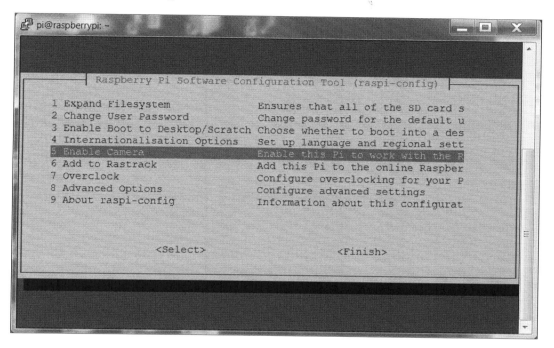

Now reboot Raspberry Pi. If you are developing from a remote computer and want to see your images, you will want to open a vncserver connection between your computer and the Raspberry Pi. For details, see *Chapter 1, Configuring and Programming Raspberry Pi*. To take a picture with the camera, simply type `raspistill -o image.jpg`. This will take a picture with the camera, and then store the image in the `image.jpg` file. Once you have the picture, you can view it by opening the Raspberry Pi image viewer by selecting the lower left icon for **Menu**, then **Accessories**, and then **Image Viewer**, as shown in the following screenshot:

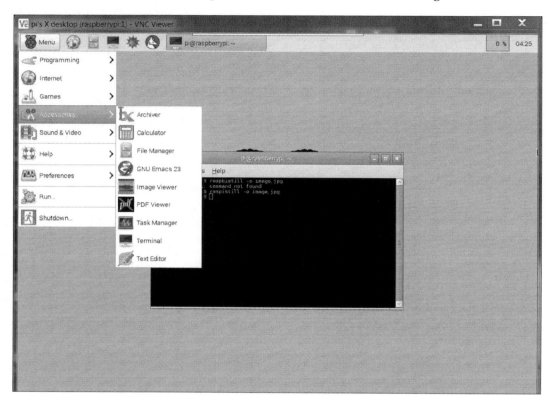

Open the **image.jpg** file, and you should see the results of your picture:

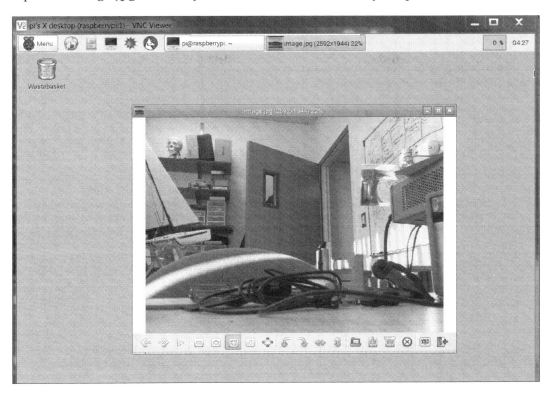

Before you can access OpenCV with the Raspberry Pi camera, you'll need to do two things. First, you'll need to add a Python library; it is called `picamera`. To get this, and the required libraries, type `sudo apt-get install python-picamera python3-picamera python-rpi.gpio`. Second, you'll need to type `sudo modprobe bcm2835-v4l2`. The Raspberry Pi camera can now be used in the OpenCV examples in the next section.

Downloading and installing OpenCV – a fully featured vision library

Now that you have your camera connected, you can begin to access some amazing capabilities that have been provided by the open source community. Open a terminal window and type the following commands:

1. `sudo apt-get update`: You're going to download a number of new software packages, so it is good to make sure that everything is up to date.

2. `sudo apt-get install build-essential`: Although you may have done this earlier, this library is essential to build OpenCV.

3. `sudo apt-get install libavformat-dev`: This library provides a way to code and decode audio and video streams.

4. `sudo apt-get install ffmpeg`: This library provides a way to transcode audio and video streams.

5. `sudo apt-get install libcv2.4 libcvaux2.4 libhighgui2.4`: This command shows the basic OpenCV libraries. Note the number in the command. This will almost certainly change as new versions of OpenCV become available. If 2.4 does not work, either try 3.0 or search on Google for the latest version of OpenCV.

6. `sudo apt-get install python-opencv`: This is the Python development kit needed for OpenCV, as you are going to use Python.

7. `sudo apt-get install opencv-doc`: This command will show the documentation for OpenCV just in case you need it.

8. `sudo apt-get install libcv-dev`: This command shows the header file and static libraries to compile OpenCV.

9. `sudo apt-get install libcvaux-dev`: This command shows more development tools for compiling OpenCV.

10. `sudo apt-get install libhighgui-dev`: This is another package that provides header files and static libraries to compile OpenCV.

11. Now type `cp -r /usr/share/doc/opencv-doc/examples /home/pi/.` This will copy all the examples to your home directory.

    Now that OpenCV is installed, you can try one of the examples. Go to the `/home/pi/examples/python` directory. If you do an `ls`, you'll see a file named `camera.py`. This file has the most basic code for capturing and displaying a stream of picture images. Before you run the code, make a copy of it using `cp camera.py myCamera.py`. Then, edit the file to look like the following:

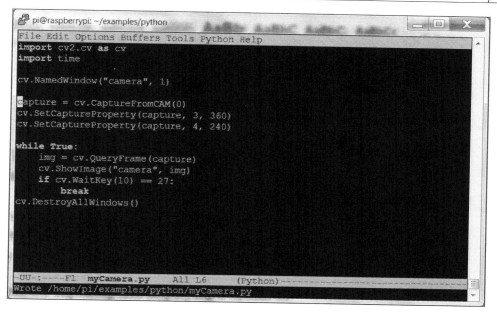

The two lines that you'll add are the two with the `cv.SetCaptureProperty`; they will set the resolution of the image to 360 by 240. To run this program, you'll need to either have a display and keyboard connected to Raspberry Pi or use vncviewer. When you run the code, you should see the window displayed, as shown in the following image:

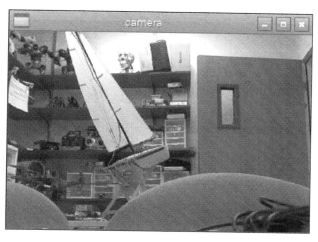

If you are using RaspiCam and don't see an image, you will need to run the `sudo modprobe bcm2835-v4l2` command. Now you can see the outside world!

You may want to play with the resolution to find the optimum settings for your application. Bigger images are great—they give you a more detailed view on the world—but they also take up significantly more processing power. You'll play with this more as you actually ask your system to do some real image processing. Be careful if you are going to use vncserver to understand your system performance, as this will significantly slow down the update rate. An image that is twice the size (width/height) will involve four times more processing. You can now use this capability to do a number of impressive tasks.

Edge Detection and OpenCv

Fortunately, one of the examples in the OpenCV Python set is a program named edge.py. The following is that file (with blank lines removed):

This program uses the Canny image detection algorithm implemented by OpenCV to find the edges in any image. For more on the Canny edge algorithm, refer to `http://dasl.mem.drexel.edu/alumni/bGreen/www.pages.drexel.edu/_weg22/can_tut.html` or `http://opencv-python-tutroals.readthedocs.org/en/latest/py_tutorials/py_imgproc/py_canny/py_canny.html`. You captured an image earlier; you can use this program to look at the edges and to also see how setting a different threshold can show more/less edges. Run the program with the image captured earlier and you will see the following:

You will notice that there is a threshold slide bar setting at the top. If you adjust this threshold up, it will find fewer edges—the edges that have a larger threshold. The picture for a setting of 30 is as follows:

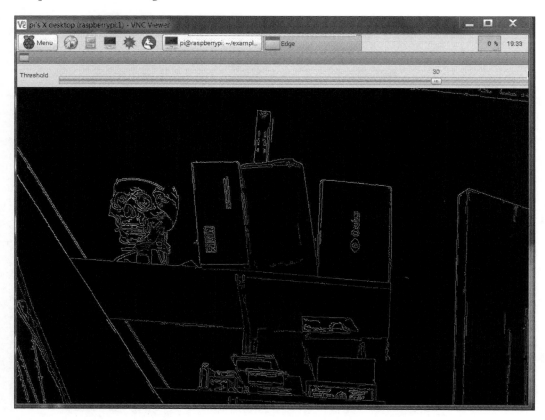

Now you can see how this process could be translated to an image of a blank floor and a barrier. The following is such an image with a possible barrier:

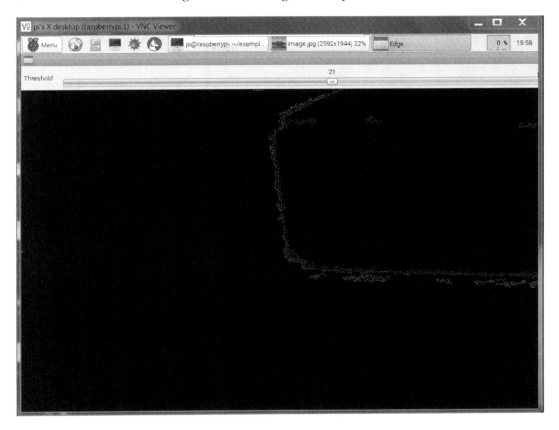

You can calibrate the distance to the object based on the pixels and the position of the camera.

Color and motion finding

OpenCV and your webcam can also track colored objects. This will be useful if you want your biped to follow a colored object. OpenCV makes this amazingly simple by providing some high-level libraries that can help us with this task. To accomplish this, you'll edit a file to look something like what is shown in the following screenshot:

```
pi@raspberrypi: ~/examples/python
File Edit Options Buffers Tools Python Help
import numpy as np
import cv2

cap = cv2.VideoCapture(0)
cap.set(3,320)
cap.set(4,240)
low_range = np.array([10, 120, 100])
high_range = np.array([70, 255, 255])

while(cap.isOpened()):
    ret, frame = cap.read()
    hue_image = cv2.cvtColor(frame, cv2.COLOR_BGR2HSV)
    threshold_img = cv2.inRange(hue_image, low_range, high_range)
    cv2.imshow('video',frame)
    cv2.imshow('frame',threshold_img)
    if cv2.waitKey(1) & 0xFF == ord('q'):
        break

cap.release()
cv2.destroyAllWindows()

-UU-:----F1   try1.py          All L18      (Python)------------
Wrote /home/pi/examples/python/try1.py
```

Let's look specifically at the code that makes it possible to isolate the colored ball:

- `hue_img = cv.CvtColor(frame, cv.CV_BGR2HSV)` : This line creates a new image that stores the image as per the values of **hue** (color), **saturation**, and **value (HSV)**, instead of the **red**, **green**, and **blue (RGB)** pixel values of the original image. Converting to HSV focuses our processing more on the color, as opposed to the amount of light hitting it.

- `threshold_img = cv.InRangeS(hue_img, low_range, high_range)`: The `low_range`, `high_range` parameters determine the color range. In this case, it is an orange ball, so you want to detect the color orange. For a good tutorial on using hue to specify color, refer to `http://www.tomjewett.com/colors/hsb.html`. Also, `http://www.shervinemami.info/colorConversion.html` includes a program that you can use to determine your values by selecting a specific color.

Run the program. If you see a single black image, move this window, and you will expose the original image window as well. Now, take your target (in this case, an orange ping-pong ball) and move it into the frame. You should see something like what is shown in the following screenshot:

Notice the white pixels in our threshold image showing where the ball is located. You can add more OpenCV code that gives the actual location of the ball. In our original image file of the ball's location, you can actually draw a rectangle around the ball as an indicator. Edit the file to look as follows:

```python
import numpy as np
import cv2

cap = cv2.VideoCapture(0)
cap.set(3,320)
cap.set(4,240)
low_range = np.array([10, 120, 100])
high_range = np.array([70, 255, 255])

while(cap.isOpened()):
    ret, frame = cap.read()
    hue_image = cv2.cvtColor(frame, cv2.COLOR_BGR2HSV)
    threshold_img = cv2.inRange(hue_image, low_range, high_range)
    contour, hierarchy = cv2.findContours(threshold_img, cv2.RETR_TREE, cv2.CHA\
IN_APPROX_SIMPLE)
    center = contour[0]
    moment = cv2.moments(center)
    (x,y),radius = cv2.minEnclosingCircle(center)
    center = (int(x),int(y))
    radius = int(radius)
    img = cv2.circle(frame,center,radius,(0,255,0),2)
    cv2.imshow('video',frame)
    if cv2.waitKey(1) & 0xFF == ord('q'):
        break


cap.release()
cv2.destroyAllWindows()
```

```
-UU-:**--F1   try1.py          All L22    (Python)------------------
```

The added lines look like the following:

- `hue_image = cv2.cvtColor(frame, cv2.COLOR_BGR2HSV)`: This line creates a hue image out of the RGB image that was captured. Hue is easier to deal with when trying to capture real world images; for details, refer to `http://www.bogotobogo.com/python/OpenCV_Python/python_opencv3_Changing_ColorSpaces_RGB_HSV_HLS.php`.

- `threshold_img = cv2.inRange(hue_image, low_range, high_range)`: This creates a new image that contains only those pixels that occur between the `low_range` and `high_range` n-tuples.

- `contour, hierarchy = cv2.findContours(threshold_img, cv2.RETR_TREE, cv2.CHAIN_APPROX_SIMPLE)` : This finds the contours, or groups of like pixels, in the `threshold_img` image.

- `center = contour[0]` : This identifies the first contour.

- `moment = cv2.moments(center)` : This finds the moment of this group of pixels.

- `(x,y),radius = cv2.minEnclosingCircle(center)` : This gives the *x* and *y* locations and the radius of the minimum circle that will enclose this group of pixels.

- `center = (int(x),int(y))` : Find the center of the *x* and *y* locations.

- `radius = int(radius)` : The integer radius of the circle.

- `img = cv2.circle(frame,center,radius,(0,255,0),2)` : Draw a circle on the image.

Now that the code is ready, you can run it. You should see something that looks like the following screenshot:

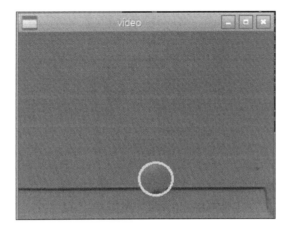

You can now track your object. You can modify the color by changing the low_range and high_range n-tuples. You also have the location of your object, so you can use the location to do path planning for your robot.

Summary

Your biped robot can walk, use sensors to avoid barriers, plans its path, and even see barriers or target. In the final chapter, you'll learn to connect your biped robot remotely so that you can control it and monitor it, without the wires.

7

Accessing Your Biped Remotely

Now that your biped is up and running, you'll want to able to send it on its way into the world, but still be able to monitor and control it remotely. This will help you in development as well as deployment and will open up all sorts of new scenarios and applications.

In this chapter, you will learn:

- How to add a wireless LAN dongle to your biped robot and set it up as a wireless access point
- How to control your biped robot using this access and a joystick
- How to use the wireless LAN connection to get **First Person Video** (**FPV**) back so that you can see what your biped robot is seeing

Adding a wireless dongle and creating an access point

In *Chapter 1, Configuring and Programming Raspberry Pi*, you learned how to add a wireless dongle and have the Raspberry Pi connect to your wireless network. This is a useful way to access the Raspberry Pi, but if you want to take your robot outside the coverage of your wireless LAN, you'll want to set it up as an access point.

The first step in doing this is to install the wireless LAN device. One device that is inexpensive and easy to configure is the Edimax Wifi Adapter device (the product information is available at `http://www.edimax.com/edimax/merchandise/merchandise_detail/data/edimax/global/wireless_adapters_n150/ew-7811un`). It is available at most online electronic outlets:

Once you have installed the device and booted Raspberry Pi, type `lsusb` command. This should display something like the following screenshot:

```
pi@raspberrypi ~ $ lsusb
Bus 001 Device 002: ID 0424:9514 Standard Microsystems Corp.
Bus 001 Device 001: ID 1d6b:0002 Linux Foundation 2.0 root hub
Bus 001 Device 003: ID 0424:ec00 Standard Microsystems Corp.
Bus 001 Device 004: ID 7392:7811 Edimax Technology Co., Ltd EW-7811Un 802.11n Wireless Adapter [Realtek RTL8188CUS]
Bus 001 Device 005: ID 1ffb:008a
pi@raspberrypi ~ $
```

The Edimax device is listed in the set of devices connected to the USB port. Now, execute the following steps:

1. Make sure that you have `hostapd` installed by typing `sudo apt-get install hostapd`. This application is a background application that controls the configuration of wireless on Raspberry Pi.

2. The default version of `hostapd` unfortunately does not support the Edimax chipset by default. So, you'll need to download a version that does by typing `wget http://www.daveconroy.com/wp3/wp-content/uploads/2013/07/hostapd.zip`.

3. Now, unzip this file by typing `unzip hostapd.zip`.

4. Make a backup of your original `hostapd` application by typing `sudo mv /usr/sbin/hostapd /usr/sbin/hostapd.bak`. This way, you'll have it if you want to restore it later.

5. Now, move the new version of `hostapd` to the proper directory by typing `sudo mv hostapd /usr/sbin/hostapd.edimax`.

6. For the next step, type `sudo ln -sf /usr/sbin/hostapd.edimax /usr/sbin/hostapd`; this will create a soft link to the new file so that it will be executed as the `hostapd` application.

7. Type `sudo chown root.root /usr/sbin/hostapd`, and this will change the owner and the group of this file to `root`.

8. Type `sudo chmod 755 /usr/sbin/hostapd` to make this file executable to the owner.

9. Now you will want to configure your wireless access point. Edit the file by typing `sudo emacs /etc/hostapd/hostapd.conf` so that it looks like the following screenshot:

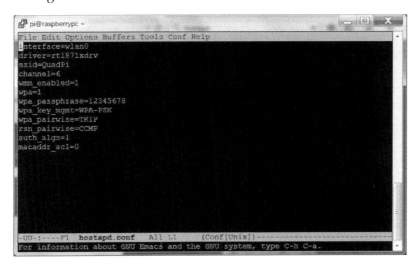

10. You'll now want to edit the `/etc/network/interfaces` file, as shown in the following screenshot:

11. This will set the address of the access point to **10.10.0.1**.

12. Now, type `sudo apt-get install isc-dhcp-server` to install a dhcp server so that devices that connect to it will be able to get a dynamic address.

13. Now, edit the `/etc/dhcp/dhcpd.conf` and add these lines:

14. The next step is to edit the /etc/default/hostapd so that this will all start at power up by adding this line:

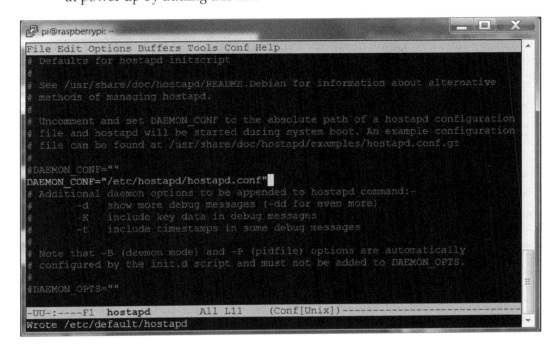

15. Now type the following two commands; sudo update-rc.d hostapd enable and sudo update-rc.d isc-dhcp-server enable and then reboot the Raspberry Pi.

You should now be able to connect to your Raspberry Pi as a wireless access point.

Adding a joystick remote control

Now that you can access your Raspberry Pi from a remote computer, you can SSH, just like you may have been doing with a wired connection, issue commands, and even control the biped using the remote computer. This introduces a number of different possibilities, one of which is to control your project with a joystick connected to the remote computer.

To add the game controller, you'll need to first find a game controller that can connect to your computer. If you are using Microsoft Windows as the OS on the host computer, pretty much any USB controller that can connect to a PC will work. The same type of controller also works if you are using Linux for the remote computer. In fact, you can use another Raspberry Pi as the remote computer.

Since the joystick will be connected to the remote computer, you'll need to run two programs: one on the remote computer and one on the Raspberry Pi on the biped robot. You'll also need a way to communicate between them. In the following example, you'll use the wireless LAN interface and a client-server model of communication. You'll run the server program on the remote computer, and the client program on the Raspberry Pi on the biped robot.

 For an excellent tutorial of this type of model and how it is used in a gaming application, see `http://www.raywenderlich.com/38732/multiplayer-game-programming-for-teens-with-python`.

The first step is to simply plug in your USB game controller to the remote computer. Once you have the controller connected to the remote computer, you'll need to create a Python program on the Raspberry Pi that will take the signals sent from the remote computer client and send the control to the server running on Raspberry Pi so that you can send the correct signals to the servos on your biped.

Before you do this, you'll need to install the libraries on Raspberry Pi that will allow this to work. The first is a library called `pygame`. Install this by typing `sudo apt-get install python-pygame`. You'll also need to install a set of Python install tools by typing `sudo apt-get install python-setuptools`. Then, you'll need a LAN communication layer library called `PodSixNet`. This will allow the two applications, the client on the remote computer and the server running on Raspberry Pi, to communicate. To install this, follow the instructions at `http://mccormick.cx/projects/PodSixNet/`. Now you are ready to create the program on Raspberry Pi on the biped. The first part of the program is the Python functions from the program you created in *Chapter 3, Motion for the Biped*. In this section, you'll create a class called `QuadGame`. This class will take the inputs from the game controller connected to the server and turn them into commands that will be sent to the servo controller for your biped robot.

The following is a table of those controls:

Joystick control	Biped control
Button 2	Robot home position
Button 1	Robot turn right
Button 3	Robot turn left
Joystick Up	Robot walk forward

Now, the following is the initial part of the code, the Python import statements:

```
pi@raspberrypi: ~/maestro-linux
File Edit Options Buffers Tools Python Help
#!/usr/bin/python
import pygame
import math
from PodSixNet.Connection import ConnectionListener, connection
from time import sleep
import serial
from robotLib import *

global ser

ser = serial.Serial("/dev/ttyACM0", 9600)

class BoxesGame(ConnectionListener):
-UU-:----F1  joystick.py    Top L13      (Python)-----------------
Beginning of buffer
```

And the following is the `BoxesGame` class, the code that will respond to the joystick:

```
pi@raspberrypi: ~/maestro-linux
File Edit Options Buffers Tools Python Help
class BoxesGame(ConnectionListener):
    def Network_close(self, data):
        exit()
    def Network_gamepad(self, data):
        if data["type"] == 10:
            if data["info"]["button"] == 2:
                print "CENTERING"
                setHome(ser)
            if data["info"]["button"] == 3:
                print "Turning Left"
                turnLeft(ser)
                sleep(1)
            if data["info"]["button"] == 1:
                print "Turning Right"
                turnRight(ser)
                sleep(1)
        if data["type"] == 7:
            if data["info"]["value"] < - 0.9:
                print "Move Forward"
                stepRightLeg(ser)
                stepLeftLeg(ser)
                sleep(1)
    def __init__(self):
        address=raw_input("Address of Server: ")
        try:
            if not address:
                host, port="localhost", 8000
            else:
                host,port=address.split(":")
            self.Connect((host, int(port)))
        except:
            print "Error Connecting to Server"
            print "Usage:", "host:port"
            print "e.g.", "localhost:31425"
            exit()
        print "Boxes client started"
        self.running=False
        while not self.running:
            self.Pump()
            connection.Pump()
            sleep(0.01)
-UU-:----F1  joystick.py    14% L34      (Python)-----------------
```

This is the interesting part of the code. This code takes the input from the remote computer and translates it into action. The first `if` statement determines what type of data is being sent from the remote computer with the joystick attached. It can be a button press, where `data["type"] == 10`, and then the statement `data["info"]["button"] == 2` determines that **button 2** has been pressed. In this case, this will send commands that will cause the robot to go to the home position. If the `if data["type"] == 7:`, then this is a joystick event, and the `if data["info"]["value"] < - 0.9`, then this will determine that the joystick is in the up position and the robot should move forward.

The following is the final part of the joystick controller aspect of the client program for completeness:

```
pi@raspberrypi: ~/maestro-linux

File Edit Options Buffers Tools Python Help
            exit()
        print "Boxes client started"
        self.running=False
        while not self.running:
            self.Pump()
            connection.Pump()
            sleep(0.01)


bg=BoxesGame() #__init__ is called right here
while 1:
    if bg.update()==1:
        break
bg.finished()

-UU-:----F1  joystick.py    Bot L61     (Python)-----------------
```

This final piece of code initializes the game loop, which loops while taking the inputs, sends them to the servo controller, and on to the flight controller.

You'll also need a server program running on the remote computer that will take the signals from the game controller and send them to the client. You'll be writing this code in Python using Python version 2.7, which can be installed from here. Additionally, you'll need to install the `pygame` library. If you are using Linux on the remote computer, then type `sudo apt-get install python-pygame`. If you are using Microsoft Windows on the remote machine, then follow the instructions at `http://www.pygame.org/download.shtml`.

You'll also need the LAN communication layer described previously. You can find a version that will run on Microsoft Windows or Linux at `http://mccormick.cx/projects/PodSixNet/`. The following is a listing of the server code in two parts:

Python 2.7.8: flightserver - C:/Python27/flightserver
File Edit Format Run Options Windows Help

```
import PodSixNet.Server
from pygame import *
from time import sleep
init()
from time import sleep
class ClientChannel(PodSixNet.Channel.Channel):
    def Network(self, data):
        print data
    def Close(self):
        self._server.close(self.gameid)
class BoxesServer(PodSixNet.Server.Server):

    channelClass = ClientChannel
    def __init__(self, *args, **kwargs):
        PodSixNet.Server.Server.__init__(self, *args, **kwargs)
        self.games = []
        self.queue = None
        self.currentIndex=0
    def Connected(self, channel, addr):
        print 'new connection:', channel
        if self.queue==None:
            self.currentIndex+=1
            channel.gameid=self.currentIndex
            self.queue=Game(channel, self.currentIndex)
    def close(self, gameid):
        try:
            game = [a for a in self.games if a.gameid==gameid][0]
            game.player0.Send({"action":"close"})
        except:
            pass
    def tick(self):
        if self.queue != None:
            sleep(.05)
            for e in event.get():
                self.queue.player0.Send({"action":"gamepad", "type":e.type, "in
        self.Pump()
class Game:
    def __init__(self, player0, currentIndex):
        #initialize the players including the one who started the game
        self.player0=player0

#Setup and init joystick
j=joystick.Joystick(0)
j.init()

#Check init status
if j.get_init() == 1: print "Joystick is initialized"
```

This first part creates three classes:

1. The first, class `ClientChannel`, establishes a communication channel for your project.

2. The second, class `BoxServer`, sets up a server so that you can communicate the joystick action to the Raspberry Pi on the biped.

3. Finally, the third class, `Game`, just initializes a game that contains everything you'll need.

The following is the latter part of the code:

```
Python 2.7.8: flightserver - C:/Python27/flightserver
File  Edit  Format  Run  Options  Windows  Help
          sleep(.05)
                    for e in event.get():
                        self.queue.player0.Send({"action":"gamepad", "type":e.type, "in
             self.Pump()
class Game:
    def __init__(self, player0, currentIndex):
            #initialize the players including the one who started the game
            self.player0=player0

#Setup and init joystick
j=joystick.Joystick(0)
j.init()

#Check init status
if j.get_init() == 1: print "Joystick is initialized"

#Get and print joystick ID
print "Joystick ID: ", j.get_id()

#Get and print joystick name
print "Joystick Name: ", j.get_name()

#Get and print number of axes
print "No. of axes: ", j.get_numaxes()

#Get and print number of trackballs
print "No. of trackballs: ", j.get_numballs()

#Get and print number of buttons
print "No. of buttons: ", j.get_numbuttons()

#Get and print number of hat controls
print "No. of hat controls: ", j.get_numhats()


print "STARTING SERVER ON LOCALHOST"
# try:
address=raw_input("Host:Port (localhost:8000): ")
if not address:
    host, port="localhost", 8000
else:
    host,port=address.split(":")
boxesServe = BoxesServer(localaddr=(host, int(port)))

while True:
    boxesServe.tick()
    sleep(0.01)
```

This part of the code initializes the joystick so that all the controls can be sent to the biped's Raspberry Pi.

You'll need to run these programs on both computers, entering the Internet address of the remote computer connected to the joystick. The following is what running the program on that computer will look like, before running the program on the remote computer:

```
pi@raspberrypi ~ $ python joystick.py
Joystick is initialized
Joystick ID:  0
Joystick Name:  2603666 CONTROLLER
No. of axes:  4
No. of trackballs:  0
No. of buttons:  12
No. of hat controls: SDL_JoystickNumHats value:1:
  1
STARTING SERVER ON LOCALHOST
Host:Port (localhost:8000): 157.201.194.150:8000
```

And the following is what the program will look like when run on the Raspberry Pi and connected to the robot:

```
pi@raspberrypi ~/maestro-linux $ python joystick.py
Address of Server: 157.201.194.150:8000
Boxes client started
Turning Left
Turning Right
Move Forward
```

Finally, the following is what the program will look like on the remote computer when the robot's Raspberry Pi is up and connected:

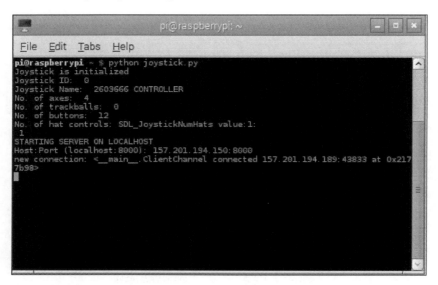

Now you can control you robot remotely using the joystick!

Adding the capability to see remotely

Your biped can now get information from your remote computer and respond to joystick key presses, but you may want to be able to see what the biped sees from its webcam. This is straightforward to configure with a webcam, vncserver, and the capability you used in *Chapter 6, Adding Vision to Your Biped*. Using this method, you can easily get a picture of what your biped is seeing, and it should be something like the following:

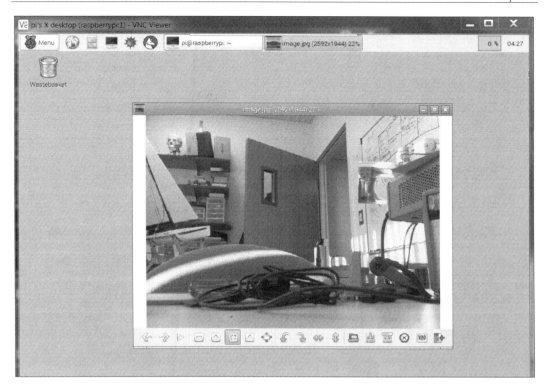

Now you can both see where your robot is going and control it via a joystick.

Summary

That's it, but really it is only the beginning. Your robot has some basic motions and some basic control capability, but now you should also have the knowledge and skills to take your biped robot much further. You can teach it how to dance, follow gestures, and almost anything that you can imagine.

Index

A

access point
  creating 123-127
ADC pi+
  URL 72
Advanced IP Scanner
  URL 7

B

basic poses
  defining 54-56
biped
  assembling 30-38
biped platform
  building 28-38

C

camera
  installing, on biped robot 105
Canny edge algorithm
  URL 115
capability
  adding, for remote vision 134, 135
C/C++ code example
  defining 21
center of gravity 57
colored objects
  tracking 118-121
commands, OpenCV
  cp -r /usr/share/doc/opencv-doc/
    examples /home/pi/ 112
  sudo apt-get install build-essential 112
  sudo apt-get install ffmpeg 112
  sudo apt-get install libavformat-dev 112

  sudo apt-get install libcv2.4 libcvaux2.4
    libhighgui2.4 112
  sudo apt-get install libcvaux-dev 112
  sudo apt-get install libcv-dev 112
  sudo apt-get install libhighgui-dev 112
  sudo apt-get install opencv-doc 112
  sudo apt-get install python-opencv 112
  sudo apt-get update 112
compass capability
  accessing 90-96
controls
  about 128
  Biped control 128
  Joystick control 128
C programming language
  defining 21-25
C++ programming language
  defining 21-25

D

Degrees of Freedom (DOF) 27
digital compass
  connecting, to Raspberry Pi 87-90
distance
  calculating 98, 99
dynamic path planning, for robot
  defining 97
  obstacles, avoiding 101-104
  path, planning 97-101

E

Edge Detection
  defining 114-117
Edimax Wifi Adapter device
  URL 124

F

First Person Video (FPV) 123
functions, importing
  URL 100

G

grid
  drawing 97

H

harness
  creating, for biped 53, 54
Hitec servos 29
hue
  URL 119, 120
hue (color), saturation, and value (HSV) 118

I

I2C interface
  enabling 90
infrared sensor
  Raspberry Pi, connecting to 69-80

J

joystick remote control
  adding 127-134
  URL 128

K

kit, biped platform
  URL 28

L

LAN communication layer
  URL 131

N

Nmap
  installing 7

O

object location
  tracking 118-121
OpenCV
  defining 114-117
  downloading 112, 113
  installing 112, 113

P

path finding algorithms
  URL 104
picamera 111
pins, GPIO 89
PodSixNet
  about 128
  URL 128
Polulu
  URL 54
positions
  adjusting, of servos 54-56
program
  creating, for controlling biped 48-51
programming concepts
  URL 18
programming, on Raspberry Pi
  defining 17
Pulse-Width-Modulated (PWM) 28
Putty
  downloading 8
  URL 7
pygame library
  URL 130
python library
  URL 95

R

Raspberry Pi
  configuring 2, 3
  connecting, to infrared sensor 69-80
  connecting, to USB sonar sensor 80-86
  digital compass, connecting to 87-90
  Python programs, creating on 18-20
  Python programs, running on 18-20

RaspiCam, installing on 108-111
servo controller, connecting to 44-48
URL 4
USB camera, installing on 106, 107
Raspbian operating system
installing 4-11
RaspiCam
installing, on Raspberry Pi 108-111
URL 109
Real VNC
URL 12
red, green, and blue (RGB) 118
remote graphical user interface
adding 11-16
wireless access, establishing 16, 17
robots
building 1

S

servo controller
communicating, with PC 42, 43
connecting, to Raspberry Pi 44-48
URL 49
used, for controlling servos 39-41
servo motors
working 27, 28
servo positions
defining 55
servos
controlling, servo controller used 39-41
servo settings 58-60
sonar sensors
about 82
setting up 83

T

Tightvncserver 12
torque 29
turn, for robot
defining 66-68
tutorials, C programming
URL 24

U

USB camera
installing, on Raspberry Pi 106, 107
USB connection
URL 48
USB interface
URL 72
USB-ProxSonar-EZ sensor 82
USB sonar sensor
about 69
Raspberry Pi, connecting to 80-86

V

vision hardware
RaspiCam, adding 105
USB webcam, adding 105
Vncserver
about 14
URL 13
voltage divider
URL 84

W

walking motion, robot
defining 57-66
walking robots
building 27
wireless devices
URL 16
wireless dongle
adding 123-127

Raspberry Pi Blueprints

ISBN: 978-1-78439-290-1   Paperback: 284 pages

Design and build your own hardware projects that interact with the real world using the Raspberry Pi

1. Interact with a wide range of additional sensors and devices via Raspberry Pi.

2. Create exciting, low-cost products ranging from radios to home security and weather systems.

Raspberry Pi Robotic Projects

ISBN: 978-1-84969-432-2   Paperback: 278 pages

Create amazing robotic projects on a shoestring budget

1. Make your projects talk and understand speech with Raspberry Pi.

2. Use standard webcam to make your projects see and enhance vision capabilities.

Raspberry Pi Cookbook
for Python Programmers

ISBN: 978-1-84969-662-3   Paperback: 402 pages

Over 50 easy-to-comprehend tailor-made recipes
to get the most out of the Raspberry Pi and unleash
its huge potentail using Python

1. Install your first operating system, share files
    over the network, and run programs remotely.

2. Unleash the hidden potential of the
    Raspberry Pi's powerful Video Core
    IV graphics processor with your own
    hardware accelerated 3D graphics.

Raspberry Pi
Networking Cookbook

ISBN: 978-1-84969-460-5   Paperback: 204 pages

An epic collection of practical and engaging recipes
for the Raspberry Pi!

1. Learn how to install, administer,
    and maintain your Raspberry Pi.

2. Create a network fileserver for sharing
    documents, music, and videos.

Please check **www.PacktPub.com** for information on our titles

43740811R00090

Made in the USA
San Bernardino, CA
26 December 2016